T5-DIH-616

The Economic Effects of Trade Unions in Japan

Also by Toshiaki Tachibanaki

CAPITAL AND LABOUR IN JAPAN: The Functions of Two Factor Markets (*with Atsuhiro Taki*)

FROM AUSTERITY TO AFFLUENCE: The Transformation of the Socio-Economic Structure of Western Europe and Japan (*co-editor with Richard T. Griffiths*)

LABOUR MARKET AND ECONOMIC PERFORMANCE: Europe, Japan and the USA (*editor*)

PUBLIC POLICIES AND THE JAPANESE ECONOMY: Savings, Investments, Unemployment, Inequality

WAGE DETERMINATION AND DISTRIBUTION IN JAPAN

WAGE DIFFERENTIALS: An International Comparison (*editor*)

WHO RUNS JAPANESE BUSINESS?: Management and Motivation in the Firm (*editor*)

Also by Tomohiko Noda

THE ECONOMICS OF THE TRADE UNION (*in Japanese*)

The Economic Effects of Trade Unions in Japan

Toshiaki Tachibanaki
Professor of Economics
Kyoto University
Japan

and

Tomohiko Noda
Lecturer in Economics
Momoyama Gakuin University
Osaka
Japan

First published in Great Britain 2000 by
MACMILLAN PRESS LTD
Houndmills, Basingstoke, Hampshire RG21 6XS and London
Companies and representatives throughout the world

A catalogue record for this book is available from the British Library.

ISBN 0–333–72467–4

First published in the United States of America 2000 by
ST. MARTIN'S PRESS, LLC,
Scholarly and Reference Division,
175 Fifth Avenue, New York, N.Y. 10010

ISBN 0–312–23586–0

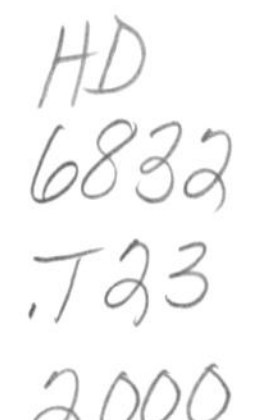

Library of Congress Cataloging-in-Publication Data
Tachibanaki, Toshiaki, 1943–
The economic effects of trade unions in Japan / Toshiaki Tachibanaki and Tomohiko Noda.
p. cm.
Includes bibliographical references and index.
ISBN 0–312–23586–0 (cloth)
1. Labor unions—Japan. 2. Japan—Economic conditions—1945– 3. Industrial relations—Japan. 4. Labor policy—Japan. I. Noda, Tomohiko, 1963– II. Title.

HD6832 .T23 2000
330.952'044—dc21

00–042244

This book is printed on paper suitable for recycling and made from fully managed and sustained forest sources.

10 9 8 7 6 5 4 3 2 1
09 08 07 06 05 04 03 02 01 00

Printed and bound in Great Britain by
Antony Rowe Ltd, Chippenham, Wiltshire

Contents

Preface

The Japanese economy worked very well from the immediate post-war period to the first oil-crisis in 1973. The growth rate of the GNP was quite high (about 7–10 per cent) during the period. After recovering from the first oil-crisis the Japanese economy performed fairly well. The growth rate of the GNP was stable (about 3–5 per cent), and the rate of unemployment was considerably low, say about 1–2 per cent. This stable and sound economy ended in the early 1990s, and the economy has since been in a long recession.

What was the role of trade unions in these periods? Did trade unions in Japan help the Japanese firms to have a strong competitive edge, and thus the Japanese economy to work well? In particular, were trade unions helpful in raising individual firms' performances represented by productivity and some other variables? If the answers to these questions are 'yes', what are the causes and reasons for 'yes'? If 'no', we have to explain the reasons for 'no'. 'No' possibly signifies that trade unions raise the wage level of the members too high, and thus lower firms' productivity significantly, although they are beneficial to the members.

Since the Japanese economy and society changed drastically in the past fifty years as described above, it is quite likely that the role of trade unions and the economic effect of trade unions also changed drastically. This book intends to examine these changes in trade union movements and the effect of trade unions on various economic variables such as wages, working hours, productivity, labour shares, etc. in these long-run periods.

Although the economics of trade unions has been one of the most popular subjects in Europe and North America, possibly because the unions had considerably influence on important economic variables such as wages, productivity, profit, investment, etc., it has been a relatively unpopular subject in Japan for the reasons given in this book. This book intends to fill such a gap in Japan.

The Japanese trade union movement differs considerably from those in Europe and North America. Consequently, it is important to identify the institutional and functional differences. One crucial characteristic in Japan is enterprise unionism, which is different from craft unionism and/or industrial unionism. This book provides readers with, first, the essential feature of enterprise unionism, and second, the effect of enterprise unionism on the working of industrial relations in Japan. The book subsequently estimates the quantitative economic effect of trade unions on a number of variables such as wages, productivity, labour shares and industrial relations in general.

The book uses various useful individual survey data for both firms and employees to draw pure effects of trade unions. One feature of our data is that we pay equal attention to both trade union members and non-trade union members. Information on the latter enables us to investigate the reasons why the rate of union participations in Japan is in a decreasing trend during the post-war period. Since these individual survey data enable us rigorously to estimate the quantitative effect of trade unions by applying several econometric techniques, the result presented in this book is fairly robust and reliable. Our final goal, nevertheless, is to present and discuss carefully our view of the economic effect of trade unions, and to show the role of trade unions in the working of the industrial relations system and the economy in Japan.

The research project carried out in this book started in the middle 1990s, after we participated in the project on trade unions conducted by the RIALS (Research Institute for Advancement in Living Standards) in the early 1990s. We learned a lot from discussions among many participants at the RIALS project, namely Corinne J. Boyles, Norio Hisamoto, Yoshinobu Kobayashi, Kuramitsu Muramatsu, Isao Ohashi, Mitsuhiro Sakamoto, Yasunobu Tomita, Kaoru Yoshikawa. We are indebted to those people. We are also grateful to the RIALS who permitted us to use their data for this project. Needless to say, we are solely responsible for any remaining errors and opinions expressed in this book.

The manuscript was typed and managed by Toshiko Goto and Yukiko Yokoyama skilfully. Tim Farmiloe encouraged us to publish this book. We are grateful to those people.

TOSHIAKI TACHIBANAKI
TOMOHIKO NODA

1
Introduction

There are two interesting, but somewhat conflicting, trends relating to trade unions over the past three decades. The first is that there has been an extraordinary expansion of the economic analysis of trade unions, as Booth (1995) correctly describes. The second, however, is that the participation rate in trade union memberships in advanced countries has been in a decreasing trend, as many authors point out. Is the real economy and the interest of professional economists moving in different directions? This proposition is somewhat similar to the question of the famous chicken and egg problem.

The purpose of this book is to investigate these two trends. Since it is vital to examine the effect of trade unions on the performance of both the macroeconomy and firms, economists have been interested in investigating it in many fields associated with trade unions. Trade unions affect the determination of wages and labour shares because of their demand for wage increases, and thus affect the macroeconomy in general. They also have a strong influence on firms' performance because various working conditions, such as wages working hours, paid holidays, etc., affect firms' cost conditions. It is natural that firms' performance is influenced by a change in working conditions of employees. It should be interesting to inquire to what extent trade unions affect the determination of wages and various working conditions, and thus firms' performance and productivity.

If trade unions were successful in increasing their members' benefits in many fields, such as wages and other working conditions, many members would not abandon memberships in trade unions. The real story, however, does not support it. The rate of union participation has been in a decreasing trend in most of the advanced countries. Can this declining trend be explained by a decrease in the benefit of being union members? In other words, has the positive effect of trade unions on wages and other working conditions declined? Put simply, do no benefits remain for members of trade unions? Alternatively, there may be other reasons why the rate of participation in trade unions has declined. We need to look for such particular reasons other than the declining benefit of union membership in order to explain the cause of the decreasing union participation rate.

Although we described that the number of economic studies of trade unions increased quite remarkably, most of these empirical works were examined largely for the so-called Anglo-American countries, in particular the UK and the US. Why do we notice so many studies for the two countries? First, English is the international language. Most economists whose native language is not English can read it. Second, both the quantity and quality of economic studies undertaken for the two countries are numerous and excellent. Fortunately or unfortunately, empirical economic studies for any country are performed on the basis of their institutional backgrounds, and of economic theories relevant for them. Economic studies of trade unions are no exceptions to this. It would be appropriate to investigate the economic effect of trade unions in Japan based on the institutional particularity of unions in Japan, and relevant economic theories.

We understand that the most important particularity in the Japanese trade unions is 'enterprise unionism'. It signifies only one union in one firm. All regular employees regardless of their occupations and professions (i.e., blue-collar and white-collar workers, sales workers, etc.) except for managerial employees whose administrative positions are higher than a certain level, belong to one union. In other words, only one union is organized in one firm, and its union is normally a closed shop. It is different from craft unions and/or industry unions which are common in the western world. We explain the characteristics of enterprise unionism and its economic effect in detail later. It would be helpful to interpret the effect of trade unions in Japan if readers were reminded that trade unions in Japan were, in principle, enterprise unionism.

There are two views about the effect of trade unions, which are basically contradictory. One is that trade unions may improve working conditions such as wages, working hours, etc. of union members, but are likely to be detrimental to firms. The other is that the presence of trade unions may be efficiency enhancing, i.e., increasing the productivity and profit of a firm, under the condition of imperfect information and uncertainty. This view regards trade unions as institutions which raise the efficiency of firms' production activity through various channels. One obvious channel is information-sharing between employer and employees. There may be many channels.

This book intends to examine carefully which of the two views is more appropriate for an understanding of trade unions in Japan, and to provide readers with the rationality of such a preferred view. It will be interesting to discuss what kind of role enterprise unionism plays in interpreting such a preferred view. We examine, in particular, the effect on productivity of a firm, and thus productivity of employees, because productivity is, probably, the best measure to indicate efficiency.

There are several other features in this book which, hopefully, could be original contributions to the literature. They are as follows: (1) We pay particular attention to the role of employees' voices which transmit employees' preferences to their employer. (2) We examine the attitude not only of union members but also of non-union members, and discuss its role in economics of trade unions. (3) A simultaneity and/or a sample selection problem of trade unions is examined statistically. We describe briefly below why these subjects are important, and how they are treated in this book.

(1) Employees make various demands of their employers with varying levels of assertion. Employers accept all or part of these demands, or sometimes reject all. They, however, negotiate various subjects and issues associated with daily and managerial matters, and remuneration, etc. We examine whether or not there is a difference between unionized firms and non-unionized firms regarding the extent of employees' demands. It is necessary to quantify the extent in order to do this. We use the concept of employees' voices to measure the extent, and attempt to examine what kind of working conditions are highly evaluated by union members and non-union members respectively to form their voices. Some employees may prefer higher wages to shorter working hours, and other employees may have different preferences. Such different preferences will produce different kinds and different degrees of employees' voices. We investigate these issues empirically.

A further question which is examined in this book, is the analysis of the effect of quantitatively measured employees' voices on the determination of various working conditions, such as wages and working hours, and at the same time on productivity of a firm. There may be a difference between unionized firms and non-unionized firms regarding the determination of the above effect. We investigate this issue.

Summarizing the role of the voices of employees, we may say that the voices of employees are treated as an intermediary variable which transmits employees' demands to employers, and creates various economic outcomes, such as working conditions and firms' performance. This intermediary variable plays an active role, and is expected to reveal the effect of trade unions on various economic variables quantitatively.

(2) A large number of countries show a decreasing trend in union participation rates, and this is mainly explained by the fact that many union members have lost the feeling of satisfaction with union activities. It is important to investigate the reasons why union members are dissatisfied with unions. We investigate the preference of union members, and examine the effect of their preference on the behaviour of union members. This kind of examination enables us to know the reasons why the rate of union participations has declined, and the expectations of union activities by members who stay in unions.

Besides the preference of union members, it is equally important to recognize the preference of non-union members in order to know the reasons why they do not join trade unions or, more importantly, the reason why they do not intend to organize a union in non-unionized firms. There must be several reasons why no union is organized in non-unionized firms. We initiated a questionnaire for non-union members, and obtained several interesting empirical observations which enable us to make a study of non-union members who are not interested in organizing a union, or who cannot organize a union even if they are interested in trade unions.

(3) Several economists are concerned with an endogeneity problem, when the effect of trade unions on various economic variables is measured based on the estimated single equation where the union dummy variable is included as an independent variable. Technically speaking, this problem is equivalent to the case in which there is a correlation between the union dummy variable and the random term in the single regression equation. It may be called a simultaneity problem. In terms of economics it says that the effect of organizing a trade union must be taken into account in order to draw a pure effect of trade unions on various economic variables. This is a similar problem to a sample selection bias.

It should be interesting to examine whether or not such a simultaneity problem and/or a sample selection problem is crucial in estimating the effect of trade unions for Japan, since several studies for other countries, such as the US, examined these issues. A comparison between Japan and the US regarding this kind of statistical and technical problem may help us to interpret the difference between Japan and the rest of the world in the effect of trade unions on economic variables.

We describe below very briefly the contents of each chapter. Chapter 2 is a simple overview of trade unions in Japan, with emphasis on the movement of the union participation rates (sometimes called the union density rates) since the Second World War, and their several institutional characteristics. One noticeable feature of trade unions in Japan is a long-run declining trend in the union participation rates. This chapter provides several descriptive explanations why such a declining trend is observed, without trying to analyze its cause based on rigorous theoretical and econometric studies.

One concern in this chapter is an international comparison with respect to several distinctions and features of trade unions in advanced countries. In particular, this chapter discusses the following subject, namely 'Who participates in the union?' Here, a comparison is made between Japan and the rest of the world. Such a comparison enables us to understand the features of trade unions in Japan more easily.

Another important aspect regarding trade unions in Japan is the effect of firm size on the rate of unionization. There is an overwhelming difference in the unionization rates between smaller firms and larger firms. The size of firm determines whether or not a union is organized. For example, 98.4 per cent of firms with less than 99 employees are not unionized, while 58.1 per cent of those with over 1,000 employees are unionized. It is noted that still about 40 per cent of firms are not unionized even in these larger firms. This chapter discusses the effect of firm size. Incidentally, it will be examined whether or not the different degree of the unionization rates by industries is related to the difference in the average size of firms in each industry.

Related to the influence of firm size, the Japanese particularity called 'enterprise unionism', which signifies 'only one union in one firm, and mostly a closed-shop feature', is briefly explained. Thus, it is interesting to inquire how a union is created and organized, and who takes such an initiative. Also, reactions of non-union members to such a movement of a new union must be evaluated. We will discuss these issues. Readers are requested to keep in mind that enterprise unionism plays a significant role.

Finally, several miscellaneous subjects such as managers' or employers' attitudes towards unions, union membership fees, union leaders, the object of unions, etc. are discussed briefly. Although these subjects are not treated as the principal concerns in this book, they certainly affect the behaviour of trade unions.

In sum, this chapter, which presents an overview of trade unions in Japan, serves as an introduction to the subsequent chapters.

Chapter 3 is concerned with the attitude of non-union members towards trade unions. Specifically, we gave a questionnaire to employees in non-unionized firms, and based on their response we collected information on how they evaluate the usefulness (or merit) and/or demerit of the activity of trade unions. If the majority of non-union members felt trade unions to be useful, it would be easier to organize a union even in non-unionized firms. If they saw no usefulness and felt no interest in unions, what were the reasons for this?

There must be a difference in the attitudes of non-union members according to their qualifications. Qualifications here imply the difference by sex (i.e., gender), occupation (blue-collar versus white-collar), age (younger versus older), and industry (manufacturing versus non-manufacturing, etc.). So which groups of workers categorized by sex, age, occupation, industry, size of firm, etc., are likely to be favourable towards trade unions.

Another interesting question is to examine what fields or working conditions such as wages, working hours, etc. non-union members are concerned with when they evaluate the merit of trade unions. Moreover, with what working conditions are they satisfied or unsatisfied regarding the activity of trade unions? Suppose that a trade union is organized. What kind of benefits are expected by the union members after a trade union is organized? Is it an increase in their wage payments? Is it a reduction in working hours? There may be other kinds of benefits expected by the members in a newly organized union. We would like to investigate these questions.

Who takes the initiative in organizing a union? Are non-union members willing to help in organizing a union? These are the next issues. Two options remain for non-union members when they want to increase their wage payments. The first is to organize a union, and to demand higher wages from their employer at a collective bargaining session through their union power. The second is to work very hard in the firm, and to receive higher wages because of their higher contribution to the firm without relying on the union power which normally asks for higher wage payments. Since it is time-consuming to organize a union and to have tough negotiations with an employer, some employees may prefer working hard in the firm to engaging in union activity in order to raise their remuneration. We are going to examine the attitude of non-union members regarding the above option and/or choice.

One of the goals of trade unions is to guarantee and support equal treatment among union members, or employees in general. There has been a convention and a belief that wages in unionized firms were distributed more equally than those in non-unionized firms. Are union members still satisfied with the above convention? We would like to examine how union members or employees feel about it in Japan.

Chapter 4 is concerned with the satisfaction level of employees about their working life, and intends to examine whether or not trade unions are effective in increasing their members' satisfaction level. At the same time, we would like to study the difference in labour turnover behaviour of employees between satisfied employees and unsatisfied ones, and to find whether or not trade unions play a role in the determining of labour turnover.

One related issue is the investigation of what kind of working conditions are crucial in the determination of satisfaction of employees. Is it higher wages, or shorter working hours? Alternatively, some employees may be concerned with non-pecuniary benefits (i.e., mental satisfaction) rather than pecuniary or apparently noticeable benefits. For example, some workers may be satisfied when they can engage in their preferred jobs, tasks and assignments even if their remuneration is somewhat lower. In sum, what kind of satisfaction employees expect for their working life is another subject in this chapter.

When the satisfaction level with working life is revealed, the next question is to examine whether or not employees want to stay in the current firm, or try to move to other firms in order to seek a better opportunity. At the same time, is it possible to increase the satisfaction level of employees with the help of the union activity? We apply the concept of the voice of employees in this chapter, because it may raise the satisfaction level. This voice is, of course, declared to employers as employees' demands.

Satisfied workers do not give any serious trouble. A problem remains among unsatisfied workers. Do trade unions play an important role in reducing the degree of dissatisfaction among union members if many union members are dissatisfied with current working conditions? Would employees stay in the firm if trade unions were able to reduce dissatisfaction? We would like to examine these issues in this chapter.

The most popular subject in trade union economics to which economists have paid attention is, probably, the effect of trade unions on wages. Chapter 5 investigates this subject. Since enterprise unionism is common in Japan, as emphasized previously, the investigation of the difference in wage payments between union members and non-union members is equivalent to estimating the difference in wage payments between unionized firms and non-unionized firms. Therefore, it is sufficient to find the difference in wages between unionized firms and non-unionized firms in order to draw the effect of trade unions on wages.

The determination of wages is influenced by a large number of factors and employees' qualifications such as sex, age, occupation, education, size of firm, industry, etc. It is necessary to eliminate the contribution of these factors and qualifications in order to derive a pure effect of trade unions on wages. Size of firm is, in particular, crucial in Japan for the following two reasons. First, the correlation between firm size and unionization rate is quite high. Second, the dual structure in terms of wage differentials between smaller firms and larger firms is apparent. In sum, it is necessary to exclude the contribution of firm size in order to reveal the pure effect of unions on wages. This chapter, consequently, describes a general knowledge on the wage determination and distribution in Japan as an introduction to proceed to a study on the effect of trade unions on wages, and suggests what variables must be taken into account as control variables.

This chapter attempts to estimate a simple wage function which is explained by several independent variables. The union variable is also included as a dummy variable. It is noted that we ignore a possible simultaneity (i.e., endogeneity of the union status) and/or a sample selection problem in this chapter, which have been regarded by several econometricians as serious problems when economists estimate the effect of trade unions on economic variables.

The final goal of this chapter is to estimate the pure difference in wage payments between unionized firms and non-unionized firms quantitatively, after controlling for the contribution of several independent variables which are supposed to affect wages. The estimation method is proceeded in the following order. First, the result on the estimated wage functions is discussed, and statistical significance of the union dummy variable is examined. Secondly, the estimated values of the pure difference in wages between unionized firms and non-unionized firms, which can be derived from the estimated coefficients of the wage function, are assessed and discussed carefully.

Chapter 6 attempts to examine the same subject as Chapter 5. There are, however, several extensions. First, Chapter 5 ignored a simultaneity (i.e., endogeneity of union status) problem and/or a sample selection problem. This chapter pays attention to these statistical problems. The estimated result can be used as a source which enables us to confirm or reject the empirical result in Chapter 5 in the technical sense. Therefore, the analysis is statistical, and technically-oriented.

Second, a new variable, called the voice of employees, is introduced explicitly to investigate the effect of trade unions on economic variables. A simultaneous equation model, more specifically a recursive model, is formed and presented, and the voice of employees is used as the first stage dependent variable. This voice variable is expected to indicate the negotiation power of employees which transmits their demand to employers. One interesting subject is to examine whether there is any difference in the magnitude of employee voices (i.e., the power of employees) between unionized firms and non-unionized firms. Simply, we are able to examine whether or not a trade union can raise employees' negotiation power. At the same time, it is possible to estimate the effect of the voice variable on the determination of various economic variables. This transmitting mechanism is written simply as follows: union (or non-union) → voice of employees → wages and other working conditions. Although the analysis in this chapter is somewhat technical and complicated, it can provide us with more reliable empirical results to evaluate the economic effect of trade unions.

Third, we are concerned with various economic variables in this chapter. Not only the effect on wages but also the effect on working hours, severance payments, paid holidays, and separations (i.e., quits from the firm) are examined. It is useful to examine these variables in addition to wage payments in order to evaluate the overall effect of trade unions because the behaviour of trade unions is supposed to affect various fields of working conditions.

Chapter 7 examines similar issues to Chapters 5 and 6 because it examines the effect of trade unions on economic variables. There are, however, several differences in the following ways. First, several different data sources are used, although the subject matter and investigation methods are common. Second, a new subject, namely the effect on productivity of a firm, is examined as a preliminary introduction to Chapter 8. Third, the economic interpretation of enterprise unionism is provided with considerable depth based on the estimated results in this chapter and elsewhere. Since we judge that the most important feature of trade unions in Japan which separates them from those in Euro-American countries is enterprise unionism, it is worthwhile to argue the effect of enterprise unionism comprehensively. Fourth, one of the most important goals or principles of trade unions was to treat members equally, or to stick to the 'principle of egalitarianism' towards their members in the determination of wages and promotion. It would be interesting to analyze whether this is still true in Japan.

This chapter discusses and evaluates enterprise unionism seriously. Is it helpful in providing employees with a cooperative attitude towards their employer? Is the employer responding to the employees' cooperativeness positively and favourably? Simply, is it true that both employees and employers are cooperative through the characteristics of enterprise unionism? It is common for employers in Euro-American countries, except for countries like Germany and the Nordic countries where unions participate in management and/or the centralized wage- setting framework, to believe in strong management authority. In other words, employers and managers dislike interference from employees regarding their management policies. Thus, employers and employees take adversarial attitudes and actions against each other occasionally. We ask whether Japanese enterprise unionism is different. By examining the effect of unions on the productivity of a firm, we can obtain an answer to the above question. We are going to discuss the economic interpretations of the empirical result based on the concept and function of enterprise unionism seriously.

Finally, the effect of trade unions on egalitarianism through the union voice is discussed by estimating the degree of wage increase and bonus which is determined normally by individual employee performance. Is it possible to say that management can determine individual employees' wage increase and bonus based only on his or her performance in production activity without receiving any influence of trade unions? The empirical result can answer these questions.

Chapter 8 investigates the effect of trade unions on productivity of a firm in depth. Sales per employee was used as representing productivity in Chapter 7. Value-added per employee is, probably, a better indicator to represent productivity. This chapter uses this criterion in addition to sales per employee. Two different data sets are used to estimate the effect. The first is for listed firms, and the second is for unlisted firms. Since the data for the former are better in quality, we use value-added per employee. Sales per employee, however, is used for the latter unfortunately. An additional contribution in this chapter is that we attempted to incorporate the endogeneity issue and the effect of labour quality on productivity.

We estimate various forms of production functions in this chapter, from the Trans-log to the Cobb-Douglas form. Either a random effect model or a fixed effect model is applied. The data for listed firms and unlisted firms are basically of a panel nature. Thus, we are able to take into account each firm's heterogeneity in quality, and thus to derive a pure effect of trade unions on productivity.

One important feature in this chapter is that we try to provide readers with several plausible economic interpretations of the effect of trade unions on productivity, if there is a positive effect on productivity. Several candidates are as follows: participation of unions in management, better communication between management and employees including information-sharing about the firm's economic and profit conditions, and keeping a high rate of return to firm-specific human capital. We hope to present the reasons why these activities are able to raise the productivity of a firm.

We add several explanatory variables in the productivity equation to control for other factors; labour, capital, capital–labour ratio, average job tenure and age of employees, ratio of female employees to male employees, years since a firm was established, etc. Several of these variables are interacted with a union dummy variable. Each of these variables is evaluated in terms of economics in relation to the difference in productivity between unionized firms and non-unionized firms. Since the movement of productivity is influenced by the macroeconomic condition (i.e., a boom year, or a recession year), a year dummy is added.

The final subject is to examine the effect of trade unions on labour shares. This is the task in Chapter 9. Labour shares are defined by the proportion of employees' procurement when the value-added element is distributed between labour and capital. This share is determined by several factors such as the negotiating power of employees with employers, investors' preference, a firm's economic and business conditions, etc.

We are, in particular, concerned with the contribution of labour disputes such as strikes and disruptions to the determination of labour shares. The labour side or trade unions can use such labour disputes as an instrument to raise its bargaining power over employers for the determination of wages and other working conditions. Labour disputes, however, are time-consuming, and in particular costly to both employees and employers because of the loss of production activity in the firm. Since competition in the industry is so severe, intense labour disputes may lose the firm's competitive position in the industry. Under these circumstances both employers and employees have an incentive to avoid labour disputes. This may be especially true when the firm's business condition is not good. Consequently, we examine briefly the relationship between the movement of labour disputes and the change in labour shares in the time-series context.

We adopted an econometric analysis to estimate the effect. The data source is different from the data used in other chapters. It is *Survey on*

Industry. Since the data have a panel nature, we apply a fixed model approach. Several explanatory variables are added to control the contribution of other variables to the determination of labour shares. Also, various measures are used to represent the degree of labour disputes, and the difference in economic implications is argued.

The examination of the movement in labour shares is basically a macroeconomic evaluation, and has an impact on the performance not only in the macroeconomy in general, but also in each firm. The determination of labour shares is the outcome of the combined effects, i.e., the effect on wages, and the effect on productivity. Since each effect was examined in previous chapters, we are able to present fairly concrete and reliable interpretations of the effect of trade unions on labour shares based on the findings in these chapters.

2
Unions and Social-Economic Background

2.1 Introduction

A fairly long time has passed since the following statement, 'The rate of trade union participation declined continuously in Japan', was provoked. No serious discussion on policy recommendations to prevent it from declining has taken place either among union members, or among outside concerned people. One of the causes for the lack of discussion is that employees are not dissatisfied with the current working conditions. We do not fully share this interpretation, as will be explained later. It is predicted that the union participation rate will continue to decline unless strong measures are adopted, or workers' consciousness changes drastically. It is crucial to recognize the reasons for the declining trend in union participation in order to prepare policy considerations. Therefore, this chapter presents various issues which are related to possible causes for the declining trend, and some evidence which can be useful to argue policies. This chapter also serves as an introduction to subsequent chapters.

2.2 Conditions of union participation rates

2.2.1 Historical trend

Figure 2.1 shows the historical change in the union participation rates since the end of the Second World War. During the immediate post-war period the union participation rate was quite high, say, over 50 per cent. This high participation rate was encouraged by the US occupation force who hoped that Japan would be a country with a democratic society. Trade unions were regarded as a symbol of the democratic political and economic system which guarantees the principle of human right.

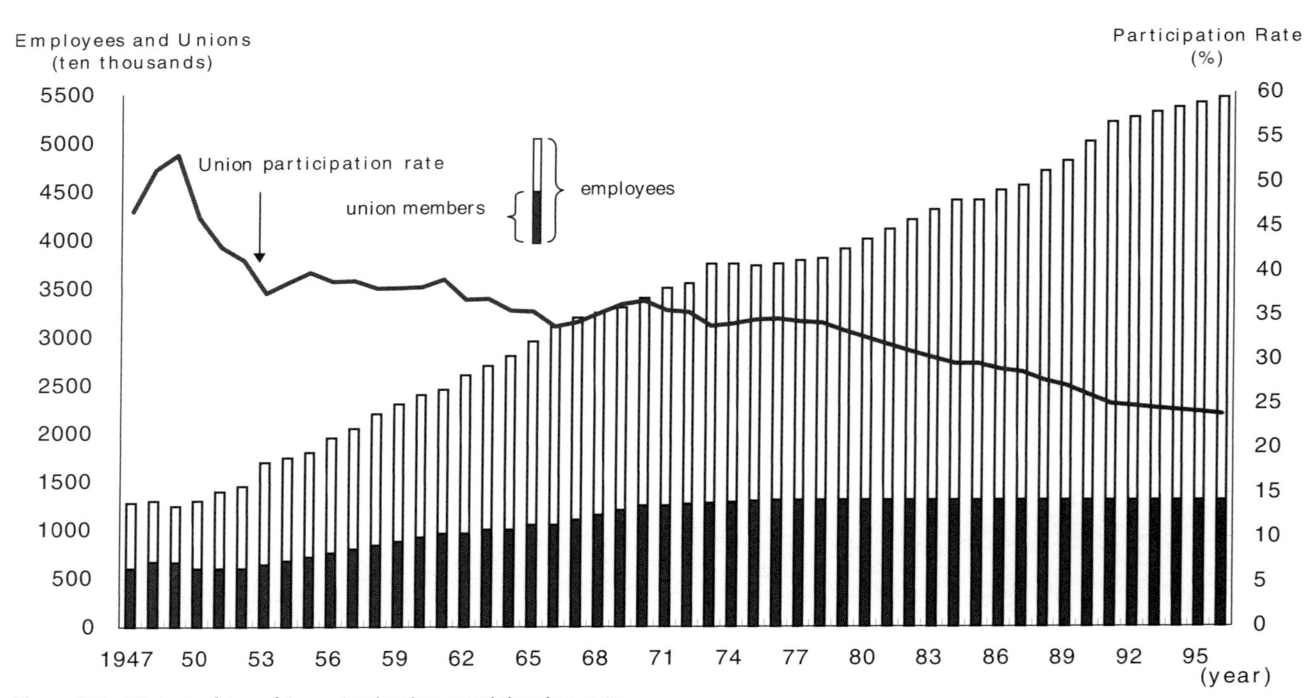

Figure 2.1 Historical trend in unionization participation rate
Source: Ministry of Labour, *Fundamental Survey on Trade Unions*.

With the support of the three labour laws both firms and workers were anxious to organize a union, and to join it. It is an irony that both Japan and the US show the lowest level of union participation rates in the world currently.

A sharp decrease, however, in the participation rates occurred after the peak rate. It declined from 57–58 per cent in 1949 to 36–37 per cent in 1955, implying a drop by 20 percentage points during only 5–6 years. This is partly explained by acute and intense union movements in this period which induced a large number of strikes and conflicts, and even some lockouts. There was severe violence between employers and union members, and even among union members, and police and security forces were involved occasionally. Such acute, intense, and violent union movements reduced the number of unions and union members, partly because some employers took strong anti-union reactions and partly because some union members left unions since they did not like such aggressive movements.

The participation rate has declined constantly and gradually since the middle of the 1950s, to about 20 per cent in 1996. This rate is quite low. Japan currently belongs to a group of countries which show the lowest rates in the world. We are going to explain in some detail the reasons for this constant and gradual decline.

2.2.2 International comparison

It is interesting to compare the participation rate in Japan with the other advanced countries. Figure 2.2 was prepared by the OECD (1994), and Table 2.1 by Blanchflower and Freeman (1992). The former covers OECD countries, and compares trade union participation rates and collective bargaining coverage rates. This is, in particular, interesting because we can recognize the similarity and difference between the two rates for each country. The latter is useful to recognize the effect of workers' characteristics on union participation.

We examine Figure 2.2 first, and are able to observe the following results. First, Japan belongs to the second lowest group, i.e., 20–30 per cent, in union participation rates. Second , the lowest group, i.e., below 20 per cent, consists of France, Spain and the US. Third, Scandinavian countries show the highest rates, over 70 per cent. Fourth, Central Europe, Canada, and Oceania show the middle range from 30 per cent to 70 per cent. In sum, we find a large difference in union participation rates internationally.

One of the most interesting observations in this table is that there are several countries which have considerably higher rates of collective

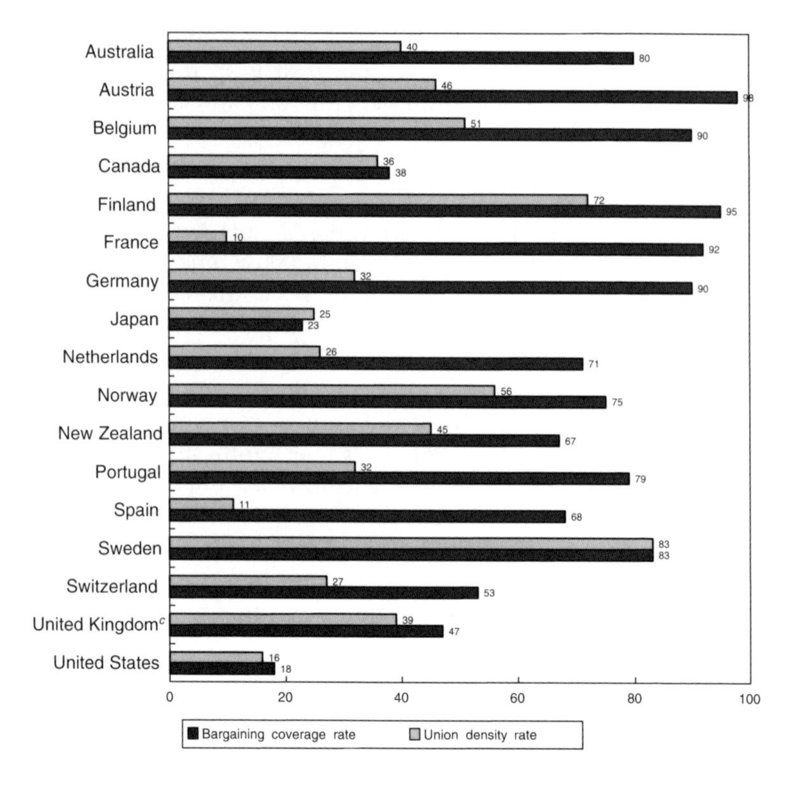

Figure 2.2 Trade union density (i.e., participation rates) and collective bargaining coverage rates, 1990[a,b]

[a] Figures have been rounded. The trade union density rate refers to the number of trade union members as a percentage of wage- and salary-earners. The collective bargaining coverage rate refers to the number of workers covered by collective agreements as a percentage of wage- and salary-earners. Coverage rates have been adjusted for employees excluded from bargaining rights.

[b] Data refer generally to 1990, except for the coverage rates in France, Germany, Japan and Portugal, where they refer to 1985, 1992, 1989 and 1991, respectively.

[c] Coverage rate refers to Great Britain only.

Source: OECD, *Employment Outlook*, 1994.

bargaining coverage than union participation. France, Germany, the Netherlands, Portugal and Spain show very large gaps between the two rates. Of course, some countries show no large gaps.

Why does such a discrepancy between the coverage rate and the union participation rate arise in several countries? The answers to this question depend on many factors. For example, the difference between

Table 2.1 Union participation rates and worker characteristics (%)

	Australia (1989)	*Austria* (1989)	*West Germany* (1989)	*United Kingdom* (1989)	*United States* (1989)	*Switzerland* (1987)	*Average (non-weighted)*
Total	54	49	33	47	18	36	44
Male	56	56	40	52	22	42	49
Female	51	39	21	40	13	24	35
Education							
Less than 10 years	52	47	37	50	20	35	44
11–12 years	56	55	26	40	21	36	42
Over 13 years	49	47	25	52	15	40	42
Part-time	37	12	9	23	9	0	20
Full-time	55	51	34	50	18	36	45
Blue-collar	56	57	44	53	30	n.a.	53
White-collar	45	44	27	42	13	n.a.	40
Manufacturing	43	52	37	48	25	n.a.	45
Non-manufacturing	47	49	31	46	16	n.a.	43
Public services	71	74	44	75	20	62	58
Private enterprise	42	48	33	31	15	26	36

Source: Derived from Blanchflower and Freeman (1992).

'closed-shops (or union-shops)' and 'open-shops' is important. Union fees and discrimination against non-union members also are possible factors. More importantly, if both non-union members and non-permanent employees, such as part-time employees and employees with fixed-term employments, are covered in collective bargaining agreements between employers and union members regarding various issues of working conditions, no strong incentive to join unions is felt by workers. The so-called free-rider problem may happen in this case because non-union members can take advantage of being covered in collective bargaining agreements initiated by union members who pay union fees, and have to spend time in negotiations with their employers.

The second source of the international comparison was proposed by Blanchflower and Freeman (1992). The number of countries examined by them is smaller than the OECD studies. Thus, we do not pay attention to a comparison of union participation rates in each country. Since Table 2.1, however, gives us some interesting source material regarding the difference in participation rates, it is worthwhile examining it.

This table clearly shows the following observations on who joins trade unions. Workers who are likely to join trade unions are (1) male, (2) less highly-educated, (3) older, (4) full-time, (5) blue-collar, (6) manufacturing industries, and (7) public services. More concretely, the table shows the following figures on average. Male workers have a 49 per cent rate, which is, higher than the 35 per cent female rate. The figures regarding education are not so different, because 44 per cent is for workers who hold less than 10 years' educational attainments while 42 per cent is for those with higher than 13 years'. Full-time workers show 45 per cent, while part-time workers show only 20 per cent. Blue-collar workers have 53 per cent rates, higher than 40 per cent for white-collar workers. Workers in the manufacturing industries have a somewhat higher rate at 45 per cent than the 43 per cent in non-manufacturing industries. Public employees show a considerably higher rate than private firms' workers, namely 58 per cent versus 36 per cent.

The above information on union members is quite useful for predicting the future course of the union participation rate in Japan for the following reasons. A change in the structure of labour forces in Japan can be characterized by the following trends: (1) feminization (i.e., more female workers), (2) better-educated workers, (3) ageing trend, (4) more part-time employees, (5) more white-collar workers, (6) towards service industries, and (7) privatization. These changes, except for

(3) ageing trend, can be regarded as the reasons for lowering the number of union members because workers associated with these changes are unlikely to participate in unions.

Koshiro (1988) confirmed this trend by his econometric analysis of unions. He adopted the following independent variables to account for the union participation rate: (1) feminization, (4) more part-time employees, (5) more white-collar workers, (6) towards service industries. He found that these variables were responsible for accounting for the declining trend in union participation rates. In particular, (1) feminization, and (4) more part-time employees, are very influential. Koshiro predicted that the union participation rate would reach the level of 20 per cent in 2000. His prediction performed in 1988 is unlikely to be achieved, provided that the current economic and social conditions prevail. However, the decline continues.

2.2.3 Implications for Japan and studies of unions in Japan

The examination of both the historical trend in Japan and the international comparison suggests the following conclusion. Japan experiences a constant declining trend in the union participation rate, and a similar trend is observed in many other countries. France, Japan and the US hold the lowest rates currently among the OECD countries. Since France has a high collective bargaining coverage rate despite a very low rate in unionization, it is possible to propose that both Japan and the US are the countries where the role of trade unions in many fields of social and economic life is fairly minor. It is possible to guess that the effect of unions would have declined in the determination of wages and various labour conditions in Japan and the US. We are going to examine whether or not the above proposition is empirically supported in Japan.

American economists paid much attention to this declining union trend, and produced a large number of studies regarding the cause of this declining trend and the economic effect of unions. Among many studies, Freeman and Medoff (1984) received wide attention both from the general public and academic circles.

Japan stays at the other extreme in the sense that no serious attention has been paid. Of course, union members and union leaders are concerned with the declining trend, and they propose several policy recommendations to stop the declining trend, and increase the number of union members. It is true that such proposals have been largely unsuccessful in increasing union members except for the effort made by the Zensen. Zensen is a trade union for various industries and occupations. It may not be an overstatement that trade unions in Japan have very little hope of greatly reversing the declining trend.

Moreover, labour economists in Japan have not contributed to conducting studies on Japan. The lack of studies on unions both in quantity and quality was serious. We can cite, nevertheless, several studies which gave some influence: Muramatsu (1984), Nakamura, Sato and Kamiya (1988), and Koshiro (1988). In the 1990s a large number of studies on trade unions and work councils (i.e., joint consulting committees) appeared in view of a very low rate of unionization and the increasing role of work councils. Typically, we can mention Morishima (1991a, b, and 1992), who emphasized the role of information-sharing among employees and employers through trade unions and/or work councils in the Japanese industrial relations system. Those studies will be referred to at various places in this book. One interesting feature among the studies on unions in Japan is that non-Japanese economists such as Freeman and Rebick (1989) and Brunello (1992) evoked the interest of trade unions.

2.2.4 The importance of non-unionized firms and the role of firm size

Freeman and Rebick (1989) presented us with a valuable study which opened a new door to the literature in Japan; they proposed that several changes in the structure of labour forces, such as feminization, ageing trend, more part-time employees, etc. are not the most important causes to account for the declining trend in the union participation rate. They presented new evidence suggesting that a net decrease in the number of unionized firms, which is defined by the difference between an increase in unionized firms and a decrease in unionized firms, was responsible. They applied a flow-stock analysis to confirm the above evidence statistically. Their idea and method are quite unconventional because no past studies showed such an interpretation.

We find that the real contribution of their study lies in the fact that a highly sophisticated numerical method confirmed a very vague understanding; there has been a common, implicit and unverified understanding among Japanese labour economists that the number of union members is strictly related to the number of unionized firms because unions in Japan are mostly 'closed-shops or union-shops'. The larger the number of unionized firms, the larger the number of union members. The reason is that most regular non-managerial employees participate in a union because of a closed-shops or union-shops system. No economists examined the effect of a change in the number of unionized firms on the union participation rate. Freeman and Rebick (1989) showed that this effect was critical in evaluating the number of union members.

We would like to point out our interpretation of the Freeman and Rebick contribution. We understand that their idea, i.e., the net decrease in unionized firms, and the popular interpretation, i.e., the change in the structure of labour forces, are not alternative hypotheses, but compatible ones. It is possible to conceive of the fact that a large number of employees who work at newly established non-unionized firms are largely female, young, highly educated white-collar, or part-time workers. It was revealed previously that the union participation rate of these workers was lower than that of their counterpart workers, such as male, older, less-educated, blue-collar, and full-time workers. Therefore, 'the net decrease in unionized firms', and 'the increase in a certain group of workers who do not join unions' are compatible. In other words, each of these two phenomena describes a different aspect, i.e., firms versus employees. It is necessary to examine data of newly established and non-unionized firms, which have information on the structure of their employees, in order to confirm whether or not our interpretation is correct. Unfortunately, there are no such data. Thus, our interpretation is only a speculation.

Related to the above argument it is important to recognize that the difference in firm size is crucial to differentiate the union participation rates in Japan. As Table 2.2 shows, the union participation rate differs considerably from firm size to firm size. For example, larger firms with more than 1,000 employees have about 60 per cent participation rate, while smaller firms with less than 99 employees have only about 2.0 per cent. Incidentally, middle size firms with 100–999 employees also have a lower rate, say, about 20 per cent.

Since whether or not a firm is unionized is crucial in view of its closed-shop system, or union-shop nature in Japan (i.e., one union in one firm), it is important to see by what firm workers are employed. Employees in larger firms tend to organize unions, and employees in these firms join them. Joining a union in a unionized firm is a fairly automatic and natural action because of the closed-shop system. Employees in smaller firms have a different story. This is the reason why unionism in Japan is called enterprise unionism. Why is there so much difference between larger firms and smaller ones regarding the state of unionism? We are going to examine this question later.

Incidentally, the survey article by Blanchflower and Freeman (1992) does not examine the effect of firm size on unionization. There are two

Table 2.2 The number of union members and union participation rates by firm size

	Total			*Over 1,000*			*100–999*			*Less than 99*		
	Union members (ten thousand)	*Employees (ten thousand)*	*Rate (%)*	*Union members*	*Employees*	*Rate (%)*	*Union members*	*Employees*	*Rate (%)*	*Union members*	*Employees*	*Rate (%)*
1985	922	3,773	24.4	533	827	64.5	245	863	28.3	52	2,068	2.5
1988	941	4,041	23.3	551	833	66.1	247	922	26.8	49	2,275	2.2
1992	982	4,612	21.3	590	1,025	57.2	249	1,105	22.5	45	2,649	1.8
1996	974	4,813	20.2	577	994	58.1	245	1,187	20.5	41	2,616	1.6

Source: Ministry of Labour, *Fundamental Survey on Trade Unions*.

reasons why the effect of firm size is ignored in Europe and North America. First, unions in these countries are organized largely by occupation or by industry beyond firm level. In other firms, workers can join a craft union, or an industry union even if they work in a non-unionized firm unlike the Japanese type of enterprise unionism. Second, the effect of firm size on productivity, working conditions, etc. is, in general, smaller in Europe and North America; there is no strong interest in the difference by firm size in these countries. The issue of unionism is not an exception to this rule. In contrast, the effect of firm size has received considerable attention in Japan, as given, for example, by Odaka (1984), Tachibanaki (1996a), and Tachibanaki and Taki (2000).

2.2.5 Enterprise unionism

We should like to emphasize the role of enterprise unionism in Japan, when various characteristics of Japan's union movements are evaluated. Enterprise unionism here implies 'one union in one firm', as was explained briefly.

'One union in one firm' signifies that all regular and permanent employees who do not occupy managerial positions join a union which is organized in one firm. The closed-shop nature implies that nearly all new employees join the union when they are employed by a firm, and that they continue to be members until they are promoted to managerial positions and are then regarded as on the employer's side, or until they terminate their employment in the firm.

One of the most important features of enterprise unionism is that all kinds of employees – i.e., all blue-collar, white-collar and sales workers in a firm – are allowed to participate in a union. This is different from trade unions in Europe and North America where trade unions are organized on the basis of each occupation and/or profession. We can observe several different unions even in one firm, whose memberships consist of common professions, say engineers, shop-floor workers, etc. This is a feature of craft unionism in these countries.

Another important feature in Europe and North America is industrial unionism, which signifies that a union is organized within an industry, and nearly all employees in the firms in such an industry join an industrial union. Thus, a union is formed across firms which belong to each industry. Such an industrial-level union is formed also in Japan. It is, however, an upper-level union or an association which consists of enterprise unions. It is best described as an association or an upper-level committee rather than a union. This association has negotiations with the representative of employers in each industry to determine the average wage level during the *Shunto* period (annual wage determination) or the average bonus payment in the industry. Therefore, unionism in Japan has the nature of industrial unionism to a certain extent.

We understand, nevertheless, that the most important feature in Japan is enterprise unionism. It has various effects on the working of industrial relations. The reason for proposing it is that both the employer and employees in a firm feel common goals: the necessity of overcoming severe competition in the industry, and the avoidance of the bankruptcy of a firm. We will discuss this feature extensively later in various places in this book.

2.2.6 Several thoughts on industrial relations in Japan

It would be useful to mention briefly several thoughts and schools which presented the ideas of industrial relations in Japan in relation to enterprise unionism.

The first is a traditional school which sticks to the so-called left-wing ideology. This school believes that the ultimate goal of trade unions is to protect the interest of workers, and thus it supports the adversarial attitudes towards employers. Therefore, its movement can be politically-oriented, and trade unions should be regarded as the principal organization which leads the country to become a socialist one.

The second is an ideology-free, or democratic socialist, school which is separated from the above radical union movement. This school believes in the principle of economic democracy, and thus wants to have gradual reforms. It supports the importance of collective bargaining between employers and employees, and of frequent communications between them. See, for example, Tabata (1991) and Takagi (1982) on the above two schools of thought.

Although these two views observe that trade union members formulate their demands voluntarily despite the different attitudes and aggressiveness to employers, there is a third view which emphasizes the employer's initiative. This is called the school of 'enforcement and spontaneity' (see, for example, Kumazawa, 1982). Employers were quite skilful in distinguishing between enforcement from employers and spontaneity by employees. Employers used trade unions to implement this division, and 'enforcement and spontaneity' contributed to raising productivity in firms' performance.

The fourth view was proposed by Koike (1983) who stresses the importance of white-collar employees in the internal labour market. White-collar skills are developed in the framework of internal promotion in the firm, and training is provided by employers to those internalized employees. The role of trade unions is to protect the above system with their employers.

Although there are several other thoughts and schools which explain the nature of trade unions in Japan, the above four are representative, and were described briefly. In particular, these four thoughts are useful for understanding and interpreting the empirical results which will be presented later.

2.2.7 Process of joining a union

Suppose that there is a worker who was employed by a firm. What options does such a new employee face regarding his choice of union status? Tachibanaki (1986) once argued this choice mechanism. There are four steps in determining whether or not such a new employee joins a union.

The first step is whether he (or she) is employed by a firm which has a union, or not. He has a chance to join a union, if the firm has a union. The second is whether or not a union is 'union-shop' or 'open-shop'. If he is employed by a firm whose union is closed-shop, he has to join it normally. It is hard to decline a membership offer in a union-shop. He can decide whether or not he joins if the union is 'open-shop'. The third step is concerned with his qualification, even if he works in a unionized firm. If he is a part-time worker, or occupies a managerial position, he is normally disqualified as a union member. The fourth step is open to workers who work in non-unionized firms. Various unions are organized based on the industry, occupational, or regional basis. The most common one is a regional union which is organized for workers in non-unionized firms. He can join such a union, if he wishes.

What step is crucial in determining the union status of an employee? Table 2.3 shows the difference in the memberships of unions by firm size. It gives us a hint about the first step. This table clearly indicates that the rate of unionization increases with the size of firm. Giant firms with more than 5,000 employees had unions at the rate of 98.7 per cent in 1990 and 94.3 per cent in 1995, while smaller firms with 50–99 employees had only 18.4 per cent in 1990 and 25.1 per cent in 1995. This is a big difference between larger firms and smaller ones regarding union status. Employees who work in smaller firms are excluded from joining unions because there are no unions in many cases. This is a particularly serious problem for workers who want to participate in unions.

More importantly, the number of workers who feel that a union is unnecessary, or are not concerned with a union, is normally larger in

Table 2.3 Union status, union-shops and impression on unions (%)

	Total	*Yes*	*Union status*			*No*	*Union status*				
			Open-shop	*Union-shop*	*Unclear*		*(A)*	*(B)*	*(C)*	*(D)*	*Unclear*
1990											
Total	100.0	63.4	(19.3)	(80.7)	(–)	36.6	(11.8)	(38.0)	(32.1)	(9.4)	(8.7)
Over 5,000	100.0	98.7	(11.8)	(88.2)	(–)	1.3	(20.0)	(30.0)	(30.0)	(20.0)	(–)
1,000–4,999	100.0	85.5	(22.4)	(77.6)	(–)	14.5	(8.5)	(43.0)	(27.0)	(13.1)	(8.4)
300–999	100.0	60.2	(16.2)	(83.8)	(–)	39.8	(18.5)	(42.3)	(20.8)	(8.6)	(9.7)
100–299	100.0	38.4	(49.6)	(50.4)	(–)	61.6	(14.8)	(36.1)	(32.1)	(7.8)	(9.2)
50–99	100.0	18.4	(8.2)	(91.8)	(–)	81.6	(6.2)	(36.5)	(39.1)	(10.3)	(8.0)
1995											
Total	100.0	63.7				36.2	(13.4)	(37.5)	(37.1)	(12.1)	(0.1)
Over 5,000	100.0	94.3				5.7	(10.5)	(51.5)	(32.0)	(6.0)	(0.0)
1,000–4,999	100.0	88.9				10.7	(9.7)	(31.1)	(46.6)	(12.6)	(0.3)
300–999	100.0	67.0				33.0	(19.7)	(41.1)	(29.2)	(10.0)	(–)
100–299	100.0	43.4				56.5	(13.0)	(35.0)	(41.2)	(10.7)	(0.0)
50–99	100.0	25.1				74.5	(10.1)	(37.7)	(36.5)	(15.7)	(0.4)

Note: (A) signifies 'Unions are necessary', (B) signifies 'Unions are desirable', (C) signifies 'Indifferent', (D) signifies 'Unions are unnecessary'.
Source: Ministry of Labour, *Survey on Communication between Employers and Employees*, 1991, 1996 (in Japanese).

smaller firms than in larger firms. This is especially true for workers who work in firms with 50–99 employees. Employees in smaller firms are not interested in the activity of unions in general, and are largely incapable of organizing a union when there is no union in their firm. In sum, there are two problems for smaller firms. First, since the rate of absence of unions in smaller firms is very high, employees in these firms cannot join unions even if they desire to do so. Second, employees in smaller firms are not concerned with unions, and thus they have no strong desire to organize a union in the non-unionized firm.

Second, it is necessary to argue the distinction between union-shops and open-shops regarding the implication of the second step. Table 2.3 shows that about 80–90 per cent of unions in Japan are union-shops, or closed-shops, implying that most workers who are employed by a unionized firm join a union. Table 2.3, however, gives a somewhat unusual and mysterious result about the effect of firm size on the distinction between union-shops and open-shops; both larger firms and smaller firms (i.e., 50–99 employees) have high rates of union-shops, while middle size firms (i.e., 100–299 employees) have a nearly equal rate between union-shops and open-shops. It is not clear why firms with 100–299 employees have such an unusual figure.

The *Survey on Communication between Employers and Employees* published by the Ministry of Labour indicates that about 80 per cent of employees who work in unionized firms with union-shops participate in unions. By combining the fact that about 80–90 per cent of unions are union-shops, it is possible to conclude that most workers join unions if unions are organized in their firms. Therefore, whether or not a union is organized is the most crucial factor in determining the number of union members, and thus the union participation rate.

Third, the issue of disqualification for union memberships is examined in relation to the third step. Table 2.4 provides a rough estimate of the share of disqualification for union memberships over workers classified by category of workers. This table gives figures of qualification for union memberships among non-regular workers. It is recognized that very low rates of qualifications are given to employees with fixed-term durations, part-time employees, retired workers, employees who were sent from affiliated firms, workers who were detached or sent from specialized firms, and workers in subsidiary firms. Disqualification of employees with fixed-term durations and part-time employees is serious because the number of these employees is very large. It is true to say that these two groups of workers are the main source of low union participation rates even if they work in unionized firms. It is

Table 2.4 The rate of qualification for union memberships (%)

Category of workers	*Qualification*
(1) Fixed-term employees	4.7
(2) Part-time employees	6.6
(3) Managerial employees who do not represent responsibility as employers	28.1
(4) Retired people	8.9
(5) Employees who were sent to affiliated firms	73.5
(6) Employers who were sent from affiliated firms	14.5
(7) Workers who were detached from specialized firms	3.1
(8) Workers in subsidiary firms	1.0

Source: Ministry of Labour, *Fundamental Survey on Trade Unions*, 1989.

reported in Rengo (1989) that only 13 out of 50 industry level upper unions allow for union memberships of fixed-term and part-time employees. Another important source is employees who engage in managerial duties and/or positions but do not represent responsibility as employers.

2.2.8 Difference by industry

One important aspect concerning unionism in Japan is a wide difference in the participation rates by industry. Table 2.5 presents the figures in 1996. There are four industries which show rates higher than 40 per cent. They are (1) Electricity, gas and water, (2) Transportation and communication, (3) Finance and real estate and (4) Public services. The highest rate comprises public employees. The public sector has been famous for a higher rate of union participation, and a stronger and normally aggressive union. The manufacturing sector stays in a middle position, say 28.8 per cent. The number of union members, however, is the largest in this industry because the number of workers in the industry is very large. Relatively low rates are observed in (1) Agriculture, (2) Mining, (3) Construction, (4) Wholesale and retail, and (5) services. The low rate in mining is somewhat surprising because very high rates of union participation are observed in many countries. The figure in this industry in Japan, however, should be ignored because this industry has almost died, as Table 2.5 indicates.

A more interesting and meaningful result in the economics sense is seen in the relationship between union participation, level of satisfaction about unions, and wage level in each industry. Table 2.6 provides an estimate of wage differential by industry and satisfaction level in

Table 2.5 The number of union members and union participation rate by industry, 1996

Industry	*Union members (ten thousand)*	*Employees (ten thousand)*	*Rate %*
Agriculture	3	45	6.8
Mining	1	6	22.0
Construction	108	544	19.9
Manufacturing	382	1,326	28.8
Electricity, Gas and Water	23	43	53.3
Transportation and Communication	161	390	41.2
Wholesale and Retail	114	1,164	9.8
Finance and Real estate	111	246	44.9
Services	193	1,383	13.9
Public	133	210	63.4

Source: Ministry of Labour, *Fundamental Survey on Trade Unions*.

Table 2.6 Wage differentials by industry and satisfaction level about unions in each industry

	Wage differential (1989)	*Satisfaction (%) (1991)*
Mining	0.075 (2)	15.3 (8)
Construction	0.031 (5)	15.3 (8)
Manufacturing	−0.018 (7)	20.1 (5)
Electricity, Gas and Water	0.044 (4)	37.8(1)
Transportation and Communication	−0.067 (9)	20.3 (4)
Wholesale and Retail	−0.021 (8)	19.0 (6)
Finance	0.146 (1)	30.6 (2)
Real estate	0.056 (3)	30.6 (2)
Services	0.029 (6)	16.5 (7)

Notes: (1) Wage differentials were derived from Tachibanaki and Ohta (1994). Figures indicate comparative advantages in comparison to the average wage of all industry after adjusted for the effect of education, sex, age, job tenure, firm size, etc. 0.075 signifies 7.5% advantage. Incidentally, we should not pay any attention to mining industries because of very few sample numbers.
(2) Satisfaction levels were derived from *Survey on Communication between Employers and Employees*.
(3) Figures in parentheses are ranks in each column.

each industry. A wage differential in an industry is given by comparison to the average wage in all industries, after the effect of a large number of independent variables on wages has been controlled for. Satisfaction level is given by the ratio of union members who are satisfied with their unions over total union members.

We find that three industries, namely finance, real estate, and electricity, gas and water, have the highest advantages, ignoring the mining industry because of very few sample observations. Interestingly, the three industries also have the highest satisfaction levels among their union members. Table 2.6 also indicates the following: 'the lower the comparative advantage in wage payments, the lower the satisfaction level', although this statement is not so strict compared with the previous statement on the three industries.

The result on the three industries provides us with one feature about unions in Japan: nobody believes that unions in the finance, real estate, and public utilities (i.e., electricity, gas and water) industries are strong, although the union participation rates are very high in these industries. It is impossible to suppose that unions in these industries affected and thus raised their wage levels. Tachibanaki (1992a), and Tachibanaki and Ohta (1994) showed, in fact, that there could be any other economic effects and reasons rather than union effect on wage payments. Such effects are, for example, the strong public regulation policy on these industries, and the strong competitive power because of higher market concentrations in these industries. These industries can enjoy regulation rents and/or monopoly rents.

How can we interpret the role of unions in these industries, or why are the union participation rates in these industries so high? Our interpretation is as follows. The reason why the satisfaction level about unions in these industries is high is that their wage levels are very high for various reasons which have nothing to do with the effect of unions, in contrast to wages in other industries. Their expectation of unions is low because they know that unions do not raise their wages. Why, then, do they join unions in these industries? The answer is simple: they do so because unions are largely union-shops which urge employees to feel obligation, and thus, they are not concerned with union activity in general.

Table 2.7 is presented to confirm the above conjecture. The most impressive figure in this table is a very small rate, namely 12.6 per cent, which shows voluntary participations in unions in gigantic firms with over 5,000 employees. Many financial firms, and electricity and gas firms belong to these gigantic firms. Higher voluntary rates, namely 42.5 per cent and 38.2 per cent, are observed for firms with 1,000–4,999 employees, and those with 100–299 employees, respectively. A somewhat unusually smaller rate, namely 9.4 per cent, is observed for firms with 300–999 employees. However, a significantly higher rate of 'recommended by other union members', namely 49.8 per cent, is observed

Table 2.7 Motives for joining unions at open-shop firms (%) (1989)

	Open-shops		*Union participation rate*				
			(A)	*(B)*	*(C)*	*(D)*	*(E)*
Total	100.0	78.3 (100.0)	(14.9)	(42.7)	(28.9)	(4.2)	(9.5)
Over 5,000	100.0	82.8 (100.0)	(22.6)	(52.1)	(12.2)	(0.4)	(12.6)
1,000–4,999	100.0	71.3 (100.0)	(7.7)	(39.1)	(42.5)	(0.4)	(10.2)
300–999	100.0	82.5 (100.0)	(15.1)	(49.8)	(9.4)	(16.2)	(9.5)
100–299	100.0	77.5 (100.0)	(13.0)	(37.1)	(38.2)	(4.6)	(7.0)

Notes: (A) signifies that they join unions because a large number of colleagues are already union members.
(B) signifies that other union members recommended joining.
(C) signifies that they join unions voluntarily.
(D) signifies 'other motive'.
(E) signifies 'unknown'.
Source: Ministry of Labour, *Survey on Communication between Employers and Employees*, 1990.

for this class of firm size, implying that it is useful to have a strong policy to persuade non-union members in these firms to join unions because recommendation by other union members seems to be successful.

2.2.9 Four groups of unions in Japan judging from union participation rates

It is feasible to propose the following four groups which have common characteristics regarding unions in Japan based on the consideration of union participation rates.

The first group consists of unions in financial industries and public utilities such as electricity, gas and water, which have very high rates of union participation. The majority of these unions are organized in fairly large firms. Employees who join these unions do not have strong motivations for joining unions, but they join. The degree of dissatisfaction about unions is not high mainly because employees in these industries can enjoy favourable working conditions even without the influence of unions. At the same time, the power of unions in these industries is fairly weak.

The second group consists of unions which are traditionally powerful. The union participation rate is fairly high. Public sector, transportation and communication industries, and some of manufacturing industries belong to this group. The group is a mixture of large firms and smaller ones. Unions in this group were regarded as leading unions in union movement, and sent leaders to the headquarters of the national level of unions. Typical examples were the national railway union before privatization, and the iron and steel union.

The third group consists of middle-size firms (i.e., 100–999 employees). These firms consist of both unionized firms and non-unionized firms, and are largely in manufacturing industries. In this group new unions can be organized, and thus the number of union members can be increased. Another policy can be a shift from open-shop to union-shop. Furthermore, it is possible to increase the number of union members by persuading non-members even in an open-shop union because it is recognized that such persuasion is effective in middle-size firms.

The fourth group consists largely of non-unionized firms, which are small in general. The majority of these firms belong to manufacturing and service industries. These non-union members, however, do not feel a strong desire to organize a union, for various reasons. Unfortunately, these employees suffer from a lower level of working conditions because they work in smaller firms. They necessarily have a lower level of satisfaction, and thus it is natural to have a higher expectation of union activity. The real story does not support it, as we examined before.

It is possible to propose the following five key words, based on these four different groups, which determine the level of union participation rates in Japan. They are (1) firm size, (2) industry, (3) union status (i.e., whether or not a union is organized), (4) union-shops or open-shops, and (5) satisfaction and consciousness of workers.

One comment is described for the implication of (5) satisfaction and consciousness of workers. It is proposed in the US that an increasing rate of satisfaction with jobs and working conditions can be one of the causes to account for a decreasing trend in union participation rates, as Farber (1990) found. If the degree of satisfaction were increasing, it would imply that the demand for trade unions decreases.

A similar argument can be applied to the case of Japan. Since the growth rate of the Japanese economy, and thus that of wages, had been considerably high until the late 1980s, it is quite likely that the degree of satisfaction with income and working conditions in general had increased significantly. Consequently, this increasing trend in the satisfaction level is partly responsible for the declining trend in union participation at least until the late 1980s and the beginning of the 1990s when the so-called bubble economy was dominant.

The long-run serious recession in the 1990s, however, is likely to have changed the social and economic life of workers, and it is possible to suppose that the degree of dissatisfaction of Japanese workers has been increasing gradually. The shift from a high satisfaction to a low satisfaction may induce the demand for trade unions. The Japanese case, nevertheless, requires one reservation. That is the fact that there exist a substantial number of unions which have high rates of union participation in finance industries and public utility industries in spite of a higher level of worker satisfaction in these industries. This suggests that satisfaction is only one of the elements which determine the degree of union participation. In sum, it is an overstatement to propose that a change in the degree of satisfaction will constantly affect union participation rates.

2.3 Heterogeneous workers and management of trade unions

2.3.1 Implications of heterogeneous workers for unions

We discussed in some detail what kind of workers are qualified and disqualified for union memberships. Table 2.4 provided the rates of qualification. Needless to say, there are several legal and practical justifications for distinguishing between qualified and disqualified in selecting union memberships. For example, first, the same amount of membership fees cannot be collected from all workers, since part-time workers work shorter hours than full-time ones. Second, those workers who are promoted to managerial levels have conflicts of interest with employers and/or employees. Third, the nature of the demand for working conditions differs by category of worker. Full-time workers want to reduce working hours, while part-time workers want to raise their hourly wages. It is not easy to present a united front to employers, if different categories of workers join a union together. In fact, the third point has been serious recently because, for example, the interests of blue-collar workers and those of white-collar workers are increasingly incompatible.

It is increasingly difficult for a union to determine a common demand which satisfies most union members who have different interests, but belong to one union. Since the Japanese unions may be characterized by enterprise unionism (i.e., only one union in one firm), as will be discussed extensively in this book, this difficulty is serious. One policy to overcome this difficulty is to organize occupational, industrial, or regional level unions across firms rather than keeping enterprise unionism. This policy suggests a shift towards the European or American type of craft unionism and/or industrial unionism. Since enterprise unionism is the traditional feature of the Japanese trade union movement, which has some merits, as will be shown later in this book, it is not so easy to implement such a shift.

2.3.2 Union fees, full-time union officials, leaders, and union objectives

All union members have to contribute union fees because a union needs management finance. This union fee has an important effect on the behaviour of employees when they decide to participate in or withdraw from a union. More concretely, cost–benefit analysis can be applied to this problem. Oswald (1985), and Farber (1986) show useful survey articles about this issue with the union objective. Ohashi (1993) presented an interesting analysis of Japanese union behaviour along the lines of this approach. The consensus of these analyses suggests the following conclusion: the higher the wage payment or the larger the number of employees, the more the number of union members, provided that the amount of per-person union fee is constant. On the other hand, if union members feel that their utility does not increase despite an increase in union fees, they will withdraw from a union, or non-union members will not want to join a union.

It is interesting to inquire into the current condition of union fees. The *Fundamental Survey on Trade Unions* reports the amount of union fees in 1990 as follows. (Since the recent *Survey* does not report the amount of union fees, it is impossible to examine the latest figures.) The most common method of determining the amount of union fees is the 'constant rate method', implying that the constant rate, about 1.5–2.0 per cent, is applied to monthly wage payments. The average monthly amount of union fee per one member is 3,090 yen. If this union belongs to an upper level of association, say industrial or national level, a union member has to add more than 1,000 yen. The sum is considerable, about 2.0–3.0 per cent of the monthly wage. Since the tax rate for withholding income tax other than wage income in Japan is 10.0 per cent, a rate of two or three per cent is not low but considerably high. This may be regarded as a big financial burden upon union members. Consequently, it is natural that they are concerned with the benefit of being union members under such a heavy financial burden.

Another important aspect of the trade union movement is the role of full-time union officials, in particular union leaders. Union leaders can play an important role in forming the union's demand and policies to employers, encouraging non-union members to join unions, and helping a non-unionized firm to organize a union, etc. Union leaders and full-time union officials, however, need to be supported economically because they do not receive wage payments from employers normally. The union fee is the source of such economic support to full-time union officials. If a union wants to have many full-time union officials, union members have to contribute a large amount of union fees. A small union, of course, cannot expect a large amount of union fees unless the union fee per member is higher. In normal circumstances a larger union can collect a large amount of union fees because of a large number of members.

Table 2.8 is presented to show the difference between larger unions (i.e., firms) and smaller ones regarding the ratio of unions which have full-time union officials and secretaries. Since the latest figures are unavailable, we show the result in 1989. It is easily noticed that there is a great difference between larger unions and smaller ones. While unionized firms whose number of employees is over 5,000 have the ratio 89.3 per cent and 77.6 per cent respectively, those with 30–99 employees show only 5.1 per cent and 5.0 per cent respectively. Since smaller unionized firms rarely have full-time union officials, their union activity may not be sufficient.

Some countries and/or firms in European nations contribute subsidy to unions in order to have full-time union officials. Unions in Japan are handicapped financially with respect to the economic support for full-time union officials. A more serious problem than the financial problem to support full-time union officials remains: few union members

Table 2.8 Ratio of unions which have full-time union officials and secretaries over total unions by firm size (%)

	Union officials	*Secretary*
Total	3.2	17.3
Over 5,000 employees	89.3	77.6
1,000–4,999	75.2	81.1
500–999	44.2	58.1
300–499	29.9	40.5
100–299	11.5	19.5
30–99	5.1	5.0

Source: Ministry of Labour, *Fundamental Survey on Trade Unions*, 1989.

want to be elected as union leaders or full-time union officials, as Sakamoto (1993) points out. Chapter 3 of this book examines the related issue. This evidence suggests that the great majority of workers are interested in working actively in their firm, and in fact they work hard in order to seek promotion in the hierarchical ladder rather than in being engaged in union activity.

2.4 Attitudes of employers (i.e., management side) towards unions

It is important to examine and discuss the attitudes of employers and their reactions to union activity. Concretely speaking, how do employers react to the demand for wage increases or working conditions by unions? For example, how do they react in *Shunto* (spring offensive)? Although these questions are important, we do not discuss them here since there have been several studies such as Sano (1969), Koike (1962) and Ishida (1990) which have dealt with collective bargaining issues.

The main concern here is to examine the following question. How do employers react to employees who attempt to organize, or contemplate organizing, a union in non-unionized firms? As we have noticed, the main reason for the lower rate of union participation in Japan is explained by the fact that there are so many firms, in particular smaller-size firms, which are not unionized. It is important to recognize how employers react to the case in which employees in these firms contemplate organizing a union.

This issue received little attention in Japan. Very few studies on it have been attempted. One notable exception is Nakamura, Sato and Kamiya (1988). We can cite several reasons for the lack of interest. First, there is a common belief that unions are not antagonistic towards employers, or that they are cooperative with employers. Thus, employers do not take a strong countervailing or anti-union policy. We will discuss this issue seriously later in this book. Second, the declining trend in union participation rates encourages employers to feel that it is not necessary for them to worry about unions.

The US case is very different from the Japanese case. In fact, there are several studies which propose that one of the most important reasons for declining union participation rates is a strong anti-union policy taken by the employer side. Freeman and Medoff (1984), Dickens and Leonard (1985), Goldfeld (1987), Farber (1990), etc., claimed that a strong opposition policy from the management side was responsible for the declining trend.

Why do employers in the US have such a strong anti-union policy? We may suggest the following two reasons. First, the US may be regarded as a typical and representative country of capitalism which clearly distinguishes between management (i.e., employers) and employees, more broadly capitalists and workers. Employers understand that it is natural for them to have management rights and to be quite distinct from employees, and to be less cooperative with employees in order to keep their management authority and benefit.

Second, as several survey studies such as Addison and Hirsch (1989), and Booth (1995) conclude that union members in the US receive higher wages than non-union members by 10–20 per cent. This difference has been confirmed by statistical data analyses on wage data, and is understood as the realistic difference by both employers and employees. Union members are certainly happy about it because they receive higher wages. It is quite likely, however, that employers judge that they pay extra cost in the presence of unions. Several firms would adopt a policy which aims at abolishing a union, or they would feel that a new union should not be organized in a non-unionized firm, as Freeman (1986, 1990) reports.

What is the condition in Japan? Although there are several studies in Japan which investigated the effect of unions on *Shunto* wage negotiation, there are few studies which revealed union/non-union wage differentials quantitatively. Incidentally, the latter part of this book presents an estimate of union/non-union wage differentials.

Besides academic studies on the effect of unions on wages, it is quite likely that both employers and employees in Japan do not have reliable information on the wage difference between unionized firms and non-unionized firms. Furthermore, it is possible to say that both employers and employees are not interested in obtaining information on the wage difference between them. One study by Nakamura, Sato and Kamiya (1988), nevertheless, shows that some employers understand that unions raise wages slightly, and thus the labour costs are raised somewhat. These words, namely 'slightly' or 'somewhat', signify that the wage difference between unionized firms and non-unionized firms is not shown by rigorous figures. In other words, no quantitative figures of the difference are available. Even in the US it is reported by Freeman and Kleiner (1990) that newly unionized firms can raise wages by only a very small amount.

It is true to say that no concerned agents such as employers, employees and the government in Japan know the exact figures of wages in newly unionized firms, or of already unionized firms, i.e., the effect of unions on wages. This may be a happy story for both employers and employees for the following reason. If both employers and employees had exact information on the quantitative effect of unions on wage increases, either employers or employees would most likely take strong action to lower or to raise wages. Simply, industrial relations may become more intense. In particular, unions could use such evidence of the benefit of unions to attract non-union members to join unions, or employees in non-unionized firms to organize a union.

Suppose, instead, that both employers and employees do not have exact information. Both sides might be quiet, because they are unable to take strong action in circumstances where they do not know the exact condition of wage gaps. In other words, industrial relations may be favourable. Unions, in particular, suffer from having no information because they cannot attract non-members to join unions, or employees in non-unionized firms to organize a union without showing such information.

In sum, we are able to state a somewhat cynical conclusion; that it is desirable for both employers and employees to be ignorant of the exact effect of unions on wages. We are going to conduct a quantitative study of estimation for the effect of unions on wages later. This kind of study may be redundant or even harmful because it may seduce both employers and employees to amplify stringent attitudes towards their counterpart, and thus lead to a militant industrial relations system. This kind of study, however, is necessary as an academic attempt. There is a dilemma here. We believe, nevertheless, that it is necessary to know the exact information because both employers and employees should negotiate based on the exact fact.

Let us go back to the Japanese story of employers' attitudes towards unions. We have little information on it, as was described previously. Nakamura, Sato and Kamiya (1988) conducted a survey for employers in tertiary industry (i.e., retail trades and service industries). They picked up only newly unionized firms. The survey reported that at the stage of before-unionization 35.3 per cent of employers regarded unions as adversarial. This figure of 35.3 per cent is considerably high in view of the generally cooperative behaviour of employers with employees in Japan. It is possible that a higher rate would be observed if a questionnaire were sent to employers of non-unionized firms. It is predicted that employers intensify this opinion because the Japanese economy can no longer enjoy a high growth rate, and thus employers feel that the labour cost must be saved. We need to examine employers' attitudes towards unions.

Finally, we discuss the question of whether small-sized firms should be unionized. This is important because there are not so many small-sized firms which are unionized. First, there are a considerable number of small-sized firms, in particular, extremely small-sized firms, in which industrial relations work fairly well even without organizing trade unions. In this case it may not be necessary to organize a formal union which possibly induces adverse industrial relations. Second, trade unions are not the only instrument which can convey employees' preference to employers. A joint consultation system or work council is an alternative system for trade unions. There are several studies such as Morishima (1991a, 1991b, 1992) which report that these alternative systems work fairly well. It is worthwhile to consider this possibility. Third, a large number of smaller-sized firms belong to a group firm as subsidiary firms to a parent company. Both employees in subsidiary firms and those in a parent company can form a large and comprehensive union which covers all employees in a group. Typically, we can point to the Toyota Association of Unions whose memberships cover both employees in subsidiary firms and those in Toyota Motor Company. This association often has a collective bargaining with the Toyota group firm. Fourth and finally, there are several smaller-sized firms which are not so healthy financially. If employees in these firms organized a union and demanded many things, there might be increased financial problems for these firms. In the worst case a bankruptcy could occur. The fourth case is the most controversial and difficult, because it is impossible to propose with strong confidence that a union should be organized. We, nevertheless, believe that it is desirable to have a union at least in order to provide a voice for keeping employment.

3
Attitudes of Non-Union Members Towards Unions

3.1 Introduction

As was emphasized previously, the union participation rate is falling. We suggested several reasons for this decline. This chapter pays attention to motivations of employees in non-unionized firms, and examines whether these employees are interested in organizing a new union, or in joining an existing union. This subject is interesting because the declining trend in the union participation rate could be stopped, if we were able to observe strong motivation regarding the movement of unionization among employees in currently non-unionized firms. In other words, even if a large number of union members quit or withdraw from unions, a large number of entries to union memberships, which would be caused by the birth of new unions or of new union memberships, might cancel out these withdrawals. If we observed negative attitudes towards unions, this study would prompt us to formulate policies which transform attitudes from negative to positive. The principal purpose of this chapter is, thus, to examine how non-union members evaluate a union, and the attitude towards working life in general.

More specific concerns in this chapter are as follows. Do non-union members feel that unions are useless, and thus that it is not necessary to organize a new union? Why do these people feel no necessity for a union? What are the reasons for incapability of organizing a new union, provided that non-union members feel the necessity of a union? Answers to these questions may give a clue to understanding how the merit and/or demerit of unions are assessed by workers in Japan.

In sum, this study investigates the attitude of non-union members on questions such as whether it is necessary to organize a union, and how they assess the effect of trade unions on various working conditions. By knowing answers to these questions, we are able to establish the reasons why union participation rates are declining. The data source in this chapter is the *Survey on Jobs and Working Conditions* in 1991 prepared by the RIALS (Research Institute for Advancement in Living Standards).

We briefly explain the content of the *Survey*. This data source asked employees in unionized firms and those in non-unionized firms separately. We wanted to compare these two different types of employees regarding various variables. The available number of employees is 847 (the response rate 63.7 per cent) for the former, and 874 (the response rate 42.6 per cent) for the latter. The number of male employees is 544 (the share 64.2 per cent) for the former, and 511 (the share 58.5 per cent) for the latter.

The average age is 31.1 years old and the average job tenure is 9.9 years for the unionized firms. It is 31.1 years old and 5.2 years respectively for non-unionized firms. One interesting difference appears in educational attainment. The share of senior high school graduates is 48.2 per cent, and that of college and university graduates is 32.1 per cent for the former, while it is 34.2 per cent and 35.7 per cent respectively for the latter. The share of senior high school graduates in unionized firms is higher than that of college and university graduates. One common feature is that the share of production workers is lower in both firms.

The big difference appears in industrial structures. The share of manufacturing, services, and wholesale and retail trade is 32.7 per cent, 25.9 per cent, and 24.6 per cent for unionized firms, while it is 9.6 per cent, 53.7 per cent, and 10.3 per cent respectively for non-unionized firms. It is worth noting that the majority of non-unionized firms are service industries. Finally, the average number of employees is 3,480 for unionized firms and 230 for non-unionized firms, showing that the firm size is considerably larger in the former than in the latter.

3.2 How do non-union members feel about unions?

It is frequently suggested that workers are not interested in union activity. This fact may be more serious than the fact that many employees leave unions, or that many employees do not participate in unions. This ignorance of union activity is particularly true among non-union members. Why are they uninterested in the activity of a union? It is worthwhile to investigate the reasons why they are neither interested in nor concerned with it. It is feasible to attract non-union members, if the problems and matters in which they are interested are handled and solved properly by a union. Alternatively speaking, union leaders can create an atmosphere in which a union is capable of handling and solving those problems and matters with which non-union members are concerned.

If we found that non-union members were interested in union activity, but no union was organized yet, it would be desirable to implement policies to organize a union. The only problem would be to eliminate several institutional barriers which discouraged the organizing of a union, if the majority of non-union members were favourable towards organizing one but took no action which helped to do so. One of the possible obstacles would be a strong objection against a union from the firm side, i.e., employers. This is a serious problem in the US, where employers often take an uncompromising anti-union line. In Japan no serious obstacle has been observed regarding this issue, as was proposed in Chapter 2.

We examine the attitude of non-union members by looking at the data source carefully. The first concern is whether or not non-union members feel the necessity of a union. The following question was asked to each non-union member: 'Do you feel that a union is necessary?' Table 3.1 shows the summary statistics. 21.3 per cent of all non-union members respond as 'absolutely necessary', and 43.5 per cent as 'necessary'. The combined rate of the two positive responses is 64.8 per cent, indicating that the majority of non-union members feel that it is preferable or necessary to have a union.

Table 3.1 Necessity of unions evaluated by non-union members (%)

<table>
<tr><th></th><th>Absolutely necessary</th><th>Necessary</th><th>Unnecessary</th><th>Others</th></tr>
<tr><td>All samples</td><td>21.3</td><td>43.5</td><td>22.4</td><td>12.8</td></tr>
<tr><td>Firm size (employees)</td><td></td><td></td><td></td><td></td></tr>
<tr><td>Less than 100</td><td colspan="2">71.0</td><td colspan="2">29.0</td></tr>
<tr><td>100–290</td><td colspan="2">73.0</td><td colspan="2">27.0</td></tr>
<tr><td>Industry</td><td></td><td></td><td></td><td></td></tr>
<tr><td>Manufacturing</td><td colspan="2">74.0</td><td colspan="2">26.0</td></tr>
<tr><td>Non-manufacturing</td><td colspan="2">65.0</td><td colspan="2">35.0</td></tr>
<tr><td>Services</td><td colspan="2">60.0</td><td colspan="2">40.0</td></tr>
</table>

Source: Survey on Jobs and Working Conditions prepared by the RIALS (Research Institute for Advancement in Living Standards), 1991.

An impressive result in Table 3.1 is that non-union members who work in relatively small firms express a higher degree of necessity for a union, i.e., over 70 per cent. In view of the fact that working conditions in smaller firms are generally inferior to those in larger firms, employees who work in smaller firms with no unions understand the necessity for a union. An interesting contrast emerges; the union participation rate is much lower in smaller firms than in larger firms as was pointed out in the previous chapter, despite the fact that employees in smaller firms desire to have a union. In other words, why is the union participation rate so high in larger firms despite their favourable working conditions? What explains this apparent contrast?

If we see the difference by industry regarding their preference for a union, it is found that the manufacturing industry shows an over 70 per cent rate, the highest preference rate. The non-manufacturing industry (65 per cent) and the service industry (60 per cent) follow. It is again impressive that over 60 per cent of non-union members feel that unions are desirable and necessary. Although the original data source shows the difference by sex and education, the difference by these factors is not significant. Thus, these figures are not reported.

The overall result based on Table 3.1 presents the following conclusion. It is wrong to think that the principal reason for the declining trend in union density is employees' feeling of no necessity for a union. This study shows that the majority of non-union members regard a union as desirable and necessary. They favour a union, and do not find a union unnecessary.

Why do they feel that a union is desirable and necessary? The survey listed eight reasons why the existence of a union might be regarded as necessary. Each respondent was invited to select a maximum of three reasons. The empirical result showed that the following three items were important sources. The first is, 'A union is effective in improving the working conditions of employees'. 80.6 per cent raised this reason as the most important one. The second is, 'A union can stop employers' one-sided or selfish management policy which ignores or abandons employees' demands or hopes'. The answer rate was 52.1 per cent. The third, at 42.0 per cent, is that 'A union can help employees in the event of discharges or restructuring in employment'.

It is worthwhile emphasizing that the most important source is, 'A union is effective in improving the working conditions of employees'. A notable but somewhat cynical thing is that they do not know the real effect of trade unions on the working conditions because the respondents work at non-unionized firms, but they respond based only on their perception or anticipation without recognizing any rigorous experience and evidence. One of the empirical propositions in this book, as will be shown later, is that the real effect of trade unions on the working conditions is mixed, i.e., somewhere between the positive effect and no effect. The effect on some fields is positive, while there is no effect on other fields. It is certainly an overstatement to propose that unions in the real world in Japan are effective.

The above result suggests to us a possible perception gap; while non-union members predict that unions are effective in improving their working conditions, the empirical story regarding the real effect of unions does not support their prediction with full enthusiasm. We will later investigate what areas or fields among various working conditions are evaluated positively by non-union members, i.e., improved working conditions by unions.

Another crucial subject related to this perception gap is that a union is seldom organized, even if the majority of non-union members feel that a union is desirable and necessary. There must be several reasons why a union is not organized despite such a non-union members' positive feeling.

3.3 Who feels the necessity of a union among non-union members?

What kind of non-union members feel that a union is desirable and necessary? What are their personal characteristics, such as age, sex and firm size, and attitudes towards working life, and the degree of satisfaction regarding their working activity, etc.? This kind of information would be useful in contemplating any policy to increase the number of union members, and thus to raise the union participation rate.

We use a probit estimation procedure to investigate the question 'Who feels the necessity of a union?' The specific model is written as follows.

$$Y_i = X_i\beta + \epsilon_i$$

$$\text{Probability } (U_i = 1) = Pr(Y_i > 0) = Pr(\epsilon_i > -X_i\beta)$$

where Y_i denotes the difference between unionized firms and non-unionized firms, X_i is various independent variables which are supposed to affect the difference (Y_i), U_i is a dummy variable (unity: feeling the necessity of a union, and zero: feeling no necessity), and ϵ_i is a random variable which is distributed by $N(0,1)$. $Pr(U_i = 1) = \Phi(X\beta)$ is obtained under the condition that Φ is the accumulated distribution function.

Table 3.2 shows the empirical result. The dependent variable is a dummy variable, namely $U=1$ or 0. Several independent variables which can be assessed only subjectively by an individual person such as 'Satisfaction with wages', 'Personal life', etc. are measured by the score, 2, 1, 0, −1, −2. The highest score 2 signifies 'strongly yes', and the lowest score −2 signifies 'strongly no'. Therefore, we rank each subjective variable by five classes.

Table 3.2 Probit estimation for the necessity of a union evaluated by non-union members

Age	−0.018**
	(2.119)
Sex	−0.203
	(1.413)
Satisfaction with wages	−0.077
	(1.013)
Satisfaction with assessment	−0.283**
	(4.175)
Personal life	0.121**
	(2.229)
Dispute at work place	0.347**
	(5.209)
Information sharing	0.387**
	(4.457)
Wage increase	0.800**
	(7.842)
Firm size	−0.012**
	(4.215)
Log-likelihood	−277

Notes: (1) Figures in parenthesis are asymptotic standard errors.
(2) 'Satisfaction with assessment' signifies whether an employee is satisfied with employer's assessment on job performance.
(3) 'Personal life' signifies the degree of sacrifice in personal life in exchange for hard-working.
(4) 'Dispute at work place' signifies whether the number of labour disputes between employers and employees is reduced, once a union is organized.
(5) 'Information sharing' signifies an increase in information sharing between employers and employees.
(6) 'Wage increase' signifies whether wages would be increased, once a union is organized.
(7) Figures in parentheses are the ratios of estimated coefficients over standard errors.
(8) ** implies statistical significance at the 0.05 level.
(9) Other variables such as industry and occupation dummies, and education are not written in this table because of their statistical insignificance.

The result in Table 3.2 indicates that the overall estimation was considerably successful in view of many statistically significant coefficients (i.e., seven significant coefficients out of nine coefficients). At the same time, it is possible to proclaim that the statistical significance of the coefficients associated with employees' attitude is much more powerful than those associated with employees' qualifications, when we are concerned with the necessity of a union.

Employees' qualifications are evaluated, firstly. Age is negative with statistical significance, implying that younger people feel more necessity for a union than older people. Since the coefficient for sex is negative, females have a stronger feeling of the necessity of a union than men. The coefficient, however, was not statistically significant.

Next, attitudes and judgements on working conditions are evaluated. 'Satisfaction with firm's assessment' has the negative value, which implies that non-union members find a stronger feeling of the necessity when they are more unsatisfied with the firm's assessment on employee performance in production activity. The positive coefficient of 'personal life' signifies the following result: if employees feel a higher degree of sacrifice regarding their personal life in exchange for working hard, they think that a union is more necessary.

Finally, the role of expectation for a union is examined. Since the coefficient of 'wage increase' is positive, the following observation can be proposed: the higher the expectation for an increase in wages, the higher the necessity for a union. The positive coefficients of both 'labour disputes at the work place' and 'information sharing' imply that the expectation for less frequent disputes, and for a higher degree of information sharing between employers and employees encourages non-union members to feel a stronger necessity for a union. Among the above variables, 'wage increase' has the strongest effect on the determination of the degree of the necessity for a union judging from its highest *t*-value. It is interesting, nevertheless, that non-pecuniary factors such as labour disputes and information sharing also have some influence on the degree of the necessity.

Summarizing the above arguments, it is possible to conclude that employees in non-unionized firms have a considerably high degree of necessity for a union, and that the variables, such as dissatisfaction with a firm's assessment of employee performance and, with personal life, expectation for higher wages and more information sharing, and a stable industrial relations system are influential for the determination of the necessity degree for a union.

3.4 Expectation for the effect of trade unions

The next subject is to investigate what kind of expectation and outcome non-union members would hold if a union were organized. The questionnaire asked various questions to non-union members about their anticipation and outcome of the effect of trade unions after a union is organized. Five alternative answers to each question were prepared, from (1) favourable, (2) somewhat favourable, (3) no change, (4) somewhat unfavourable, and (5) unfavourable. By combining the first two answers, and the last three, respectively, we call (1) favourable (i.e., achieving better conditions) for the first, and (2) unfavourable (i.e., achieving worse condition or no change) for the second, respectively. Table 3.3 shows the empirical result.

What is the expectation for wages? About 50 per cent of non-union members anticipate that an increase in wages would be obtained after a union is organized. This figure is interesting and surprising because no

Table 3.3 The possible effect of trade unions if a union is organized (%)

	Favourable (better conditions)	*Unfavourable (worse conditions)*
Wages		
Total	51.5	48.5
Male	53.3	46.7
Female	49.1	50.9
Disputes		
Total	33.1	66.9
Male	35.8	64.2
Female	31.8	68.2
Information sharing		
Total	61.8	38.2
Male	64.2	35.8
Female	59.5	40.5
Welfare		
Total	61.5	38.6
Male	65.9	34.1
Female	57.0	43.0
Reduction in working hours		
Total	39.1	60.9
Male	42.5	57.5
Female	34.1	65.9

Source: Survey on Jobs and Working Conditions prepared by RIALS, 1991.

concrete and visible evidence is known among non-union members. In other words, non-union members have no rigorous empirical foundations which support their vague anticipations. We do not know the reason why the response is divided so sharply. One reason may be that non-union members already know what actually takes place in unionized firms, while another reason may be that they regard trade unions as powerless.

Only 33.1 per cent of non-union members predict that the number of labour disputes will decrease. The impressive figure here is the high rate of respondents who do not predict a decrease in labour disputes. And for information sharing more than 60 per cent respond favourably. It is somewhat contradictory to have the above two features; the effect on labour disputes is negative, while the effect on information sharing is positive.

About 62.2 per cent of non-union members find that the system for welfare prepared by firms would improve, implying that employees regard a union as an institution which is able to take an initiative to improve the level of welfare for employees.

A somewhat surprising outcome appeared regarding a reduction in working hours. Only 40 per cent of non-union members predict that working hours would be reduced. The majority feel that it would be difficult to reduce working hours even if a union is organized. The reduction in working hours was one of the national goals in the past ten years in view of longer working hours in Japan compared with other industrialized countries. Employees do not predict that it would be easy to reduce working hours for various reasons.

Another interesting result can be observed by looking at the relative rank of the importance among various matters and items which should be evaluated when a union is organized. Non-union members judge the issue of wages and bonuses as the top priority with which a union should deal. 60.5 per cent of non-union members raise the issue of wages and bonuses. The second priority is 48.9 per cent on improvement in the firm's welfare system, and the third is 30.3 per cent on reduction in working hours. The other issues and matters follow after these three. In total, there are nine issues and matters. Although the above three matters are regarded as the important ones by non-union members, they do not predict that their demands would be fulfilled even if a union was organized. For example, they anticipate that the issue associated with wages and bonuses would be achieved only with the fourth rank among the nine issues, and the one associated with reduction in working hours with the fifth rank. In sum, there is a serious perception gap, i.e., a gap between expectation and reality regarding the effect of trade unions.

One overall conclusion based on the above analysis suggests that the evaluation made by non-union members on the effect of trade unions on various issues, matters and working conditions is divided almost evenly among non-union members. About half of them find that a union can have a positive effect, while the other half do not share this opinion. One of the reasons why there is no strong trend in organizing a union among non-union members arises from this fact; about half of them do not anticipate the positive effect of a union, and thus they do not hold a strong incentive to organize one. On the other hand, it seems that about 50 per cent of non-union members are favourable about the effect of unions, and thus that there remains a hope of increasing the union participation rate if these 50 per cent become active in organizing a union.

The previous chapter suggested the following phenomena which could account for the declining trend of unionization: (1) more female labour forces, (2) more highly educated workers, (3) more part-time employees, (4) more white-collar workers, (5) towards service industries, (6) privatization. The above six phenomena tell the recent changes in the industrial structure, or the labour force structure, that have taken place in Japan. It is correct that these phenomena can explain the increase in the number of workers who do not join trade unions, and who work in firms with no unions. As Freeman and Rebick (1989) proposed, there is a trend of an increasing number of non-unionized firms, and the majority of newly established firms are non-unionized.

We believe that there is a missing element here: we do not know the reason why there is no significant movement of unionizing non-unionized firms. It is apparent that non-unionized firms continue to be non-unionized. Why is there such a trend?

We have already provided one answer to this question: about half of non-union members do not find or expect any significant positive effect of a union to improve working conditions. It is likely that those people are not enthusiastic about unionization. The next question is, who or what kind of people find no significant positive effect of a union? Are they male or female, blue-collar or white-collar, educated or less-educated, or working in the manufacturing or the service industry? On the other hand, who finds the significant positive effect? Answers to these questions also are useful to interpret the issue of unionization.

Table 3.3 gave us an interesting observation regarding the difference between men and women; female non-union members judge unions more severely, and thus less optimistically than male non-union members. One example is that 57.0 per cent of female non-union members evaluate the effect of the role of unions on company welfare positively, while 65.9 per cent of men do. Women are more unfavourable than men about the effect of unions on a firm's welfare system. The second example is that 53.3 per cent of men feel that wages will increase, as against 49.1 per cent of females. The third example is that only 34.1 per cent of female non-union members find that working hours will decrease, while the figure for men is 42.5 per cent. In general, female non-union members do not expect that more favourable working conditions would be achieved even if a union were organized. Since the proportion of female employees is in an increasing trend, this severe evaluation by females may be an obstacle against the increase in union members and thus unionization movement.

Table 3.4 shows some interesting differences by industry, occupation or firm size regarding the possible effects of a union. It is noted that Table 3.4 gives only figures in the case in which there are some differences between 'favourable' and 'unfavourable'. In other words, on matters and issues which are not shown in this table there is little difference between favourable and unfavourable.

The difference by industry is examined first. The overall result suggests that non-union employees who work in the non-manufacturing industries, in particular the service industries, predict more severe outcomes than those in the manufacturing industries. Although both industries show figures higher than 60 per cent with respect to the effect on company welfare, 'favourable' in the manufacturing industries is 60.7 per cent on wage increases, while it is under 50 per cent, namely 47.7 per cent, in the service industries. A similar story holds for the effect on working hours. Since Japanese society is currently experiencing an increasing trend towards more service industries, this finding is not encouraging, at least for the unionization movement.

Next, the difference by occupation is examined. The general impression based on this table is that the expectation by white-collar workers is more unfavourable than that by blue-collar workers. For example, more than 70 per cent of production workers (i.e., blue-collar workers) find that an increase in wages will be observed, while the figures for sales, clerical and managerial, and research and development workers are 55.9 per cent, 48.5 per cent and 42.5 per cent, respectively. All white-collar workers' figures are below 50 per cent; the majority of white-collar workers do not expect any increase in wages, even if a union is organized.

Table 3.4 The possible effect of trade unions if a union is organized. Its difference by industry, occupation and firm size evaluated by men (%)

	Favourable	*Unfavourable*
Manufacturing industries		
Welfare	68.6	31.4
Wages	60.7	39.3
Working hours	64.7	35.3
Services industry		
Welfare	65.0	35.0
Wages	47.7	52.3
Working hours	41.2	58.8
Blue-collar		
Wages	70.5	29.5
Working hours	63.6	36.4
Sales		
Wages	55.9	44.1
Working hours	39.7	60.3
Clerical and managerial		
Wages	48.5	51.5
Working hours	42.6	57.4
Research and development		
Wages	45.2	54.8
Working hours	41.4	58.6
Firm size (300–499)		
Working hours	63.9	36.1
Firm size (less than 300)		
Working hours	36.5	63.5

Note: The original source showed more detailed figures for various criteria. The figures here are written only in the case in which there is a difference between favourable and unfavourable.
Source: *Survey on Jobs and Working Conditions* prepared by RIALS, 1991.

Finally, the difference by firm size is discussed. There is a striking difference between workers in smaller firms (i.e., a firm with less than 300 employees) and those in medium size firms (i.e., a firm with 300–499 employees): only 36.5 per cent of the latter say resulting decreasing working hours, while the figure for the former is 63.9 per cent. Employees in smaller firms are sceptical about the effect of a union. This is true also for female attitudes regarding wage increases, although figures are not given in Table 3.4. It is possible to conclude that non-union members in smaller firms are not so enthusiastic about the effect of a union on various working conditions.

It should be useful to summarize the overall findings regarding the difference by industry, occupation and firm size. First, the overall assessment on the effect of a union by non-union members shows that 'favourable' and 'unfavourable' are around the figure of 50 per cent. The estimated figure hardly goes beyond 80 per cent or below 30 per cent. It implies that the assessment is divided almost equally between favourable and unfavourable, very roughly speaking.

Second, and more important, females are more sceptical than males regarding the effect of a union. This is true also for employees in the non-manufacturing industries in comparison with the manufacturing industries, and for white-collar workers in comparison with blue-collar employees, respectively. As was found previously, females, employees in the non-manufacturing industries, and white-collar workers are less likely to participate in trade unions than are males, employees in the manufacturing industries, and blue-collar workers. Since non-union members in the former group are sceptical with respect to the effect of a union, it is hard to expect that those workers are interested in joining unions, or in organizing a union.

A somewhat disappointing finding is that non-union members in smaller firms are more doubtful regarding the effect of unions than those in larger firms. Since working conditions such as wages, working hours, and firm's welfare system are inferior, in general, in smaller firms, employees in these firms are entitled to be more demanding to their employers. However, this study found that they were, in fact, more sceptical and doubtful of unions. One of the reasons for this scepticism and less demanding attitudes arises from their fear that too much demand and/or more aggressive attitude would result in providing a firm with serious trouble, and consequently in the worst case ending as an eventual bankruptcy. We will discuss these issues again later.

The next subject with which we are concerned is how non-union members evaluate or assess a union itself. Are they favourable or unfavourable towards a union, or more specifically do they find that a union is reliable, or not? Table 3.5 shows the summary statistics.

Table 3.5 provides us with the following observations. First, the evaluation by females is impressive because 'reliable' is 24.5 per cent, while 'unreliable' is 12.4 per cent. Second, the degree of 'unreliable' increases with the higher educational attainment. 'Reliable' is higher than 'unreliable' for high school graduates, while the inverse relationship is observed for university graduates. Third, 'reliable' is much higher, i.e., 31.8 per cent, than 'unreliable', i.e., 9.1 per cent for production workers, i.e., blue-collar workers. The gap declines for sales workers. The inverse

Table 3.5 Reliability and capability of unions (%)

Reliability	*Reliable*	*Unreliable*
Female employees	24.5	12.4
Education		
(male graduates)		
High school	17.3	12.8
Junior college	19.7	17.1
University	15.8	18.1
Occupation		
(male employees)		
Production workers	31.8	9.1
Sales	21.1	14.7
Clerical and managerial	11.8	15.4
Research and development	17.8	24.7
Industry		
Manufacturing	33.3	11.8
Non-manufacturing	16.4	16.2
Services	17.3	15.8
Capability	*Strong*	*Weak*
Sex		
Total	19.0	20.0
Male	19.0	20.0
Female	24.5	17.1
Education		
High school	19.2	21.2
Junior college	21.1	21.2
University	18.5	19.2
Industry		
Manufacturing	21.6	27.5
Non-manufacturing	18.8	18.8
Services	21.9	18.5

Sources: Survey on Jobs and Working Conditions, prepared by RIALS, 1991.

relationship is observed both for clerical and managerial workers, and workers who engage in research and development. The contrast due to education and occupation is quite enormous and impressive. Fourth, 'reliable' is three times higher than 'unreliable' in the manufacturing industries, 33.9 per cent versus 11.8 per cent. The gap between them decreases drastically in other industries. It is nearly zero in the non-manufacturing industries and service industries.

The bottom part of Table 3.5 gives figures on the strength and weakness of unions. The following question was raised: 'Are unions strong and powerful, or weak and powerless?' We observe the following results based on this table. First, women find more strength, namely

24.5 per cent, than weakness, namely 17.7 per cent, with respect to the union power, while men show a nearly equal judgement on strength versus weakness. There is an interesting contrast between the effect of a union and the power of a union, which is judged by female assessment, because females found a less obvious positive effect of unions but stronger power of unions. Second, the difference in educational attainment, namely high school, junior college, or university graduates, does not give us very different results in the evaluation concerning the strength of unions. Third, 21.6 per cent of manufacturing employees find that unions are strong and powerful, while 27.5 per cent of them understand that unions are weak and powerless. This is again a contrast between the effect and the power. In the service industries 21.9 per cent say 'strong', while 18.5 per cent say 'weak'. Again a contrast appeared between the effect and the power. The figure in the non-manufacturing industries is nearly the same between 'strong' and 'weak'.

The overall result based on the bottom part of Table 3.5 suggests the following. The increasing share of employees who are classified by sex, industry, occupation and education (i.e., females, service industries, white-collars and highly educated) in total labour forces implies that the power of unions becomes weaker, although it is somewhat risky to propose it with strong confidence.

3.5 Reasons for the absence of a strong unionization movement

The next question is to investigate the reasons for weak unionization, i.e., no strong movement of creating or organizing a union in non-unionized firms is seen in the real world. The survey posed one question: 'Why do you think that a union is not organized in non-union firms?' Each respondent chose two answers among the given five alternative answers. The most important cause according to non-union members' judgement is, 'There is nobody who takes an initiative, and thus who wants to be a leader to organize a union.' About 70 per cent of non-union members raised this answer. The next reasons which received only 20 per cent votes are, 'Employers take an attitude against unionization', 'We cannot find any merit which cancels out the burden of union fees', 'We do not know how to organize a union.' These answers suggest that the lack of leaders among non-union members who take an initiative is an overwhelmingly important reason.

Since we do not ask what are the attitudes of employers in this survey, it is impossible to compare employees' and employers' attitudes. The above result, nevertheless, implies that non-union members regard the main cause of weak unionization movement as their own problem, and thus not as outside interference.

Nakamura, Sato and Kamiya (1988) proposed the following three alternative types with respect to the ways and procedures of organizing a union; (1) visiting non-unionized firms and persuading by outside union leaders, (2) taking own internal initiative and receiving help from outside, and (3) no strict internal initiative. They found that (2) taking own internal initiative and receiving help from outside was the most important, implying that most new unions are organized, first, by internal initiative, and subsequently with the help of outside union members. Most new unions are organized in this way.

The current study, however, shows the lack of internal initiative, i.e., the lack of leaders who take an initial action. Although in reality, as was proposed by Nakamura, Sato and Kamiya, the view that 'taking own internal initiative and receiving help from outside' is vital to organize a union, non-union members who do not organize a union find that no person takes an initial action.

Nakamura, Sato, and Kamiya (1988) prefer the first view, namely 'visiting and persuading by outsiders', in order to create and organize a new union, although they admit that this method has not worked very well because leaders at the upper level of unions such as industrial unions were neither anxious nor competent. We do not share their preference because we believe that internal initiative is more important than outside persuasion in order to organize a new union. The empirical result, however, based on this chapter is negative about it.

Why are non-union members uninterested in taking any action, or in becoming a union leader? It is necessary to recognize the reasons why so many employees are not interested in taking an initiative to organize a new union, or in becoming a union leader. One immediate clue to answering to this question can be found in a recent social trend in Japan: people are less and less enthusiastic in sacrificing their individual time and energy. They are not interested in achieving a collective goal by spending their own time and skill. In other words, individualism, which is concerned only with his or her own interest and achievement, is stronger and stronger. Under this trend, it is easy to see why few people are interested in taking the initiative to organize a union, or to become a union leader. Engaging in such tasks would force an individual to sacrifice individual time and energy.

Besides this general trend of individualism we have to raise a more apparent economic reason: Japanese people achieved a considerably high living standard owing to the increase in incomes and wages, although several specialists do not agree with this idea. The latter opinion claims that the real living standard is not so high in view of a fairly high level of prices in goods and land. It is certainly true, nevertheless, that the level of nominal incomes and wages is much higher currently than that some thirty or forty years ago. There is little incentive to demand more wages with the help of union powers. A large number of people feel that it is not their business to organize a union.

Another interesting reason, somewhat contradictory to the previous one, is that there is an overcommitment to working life felt by employees in Japan. As was proposed previously, about 70 per cent of employees find that they work too hard at the expense of their personal and private lives. An immediate contradiction emerges between the high level of incomes and wages, and the overcommitment to working life, because people do not want to work hard if they have high wages.

Two possible answers to solve this apparent contradiction may be suggested. First, since human desire to receive more income and wage for seeking the highest living standard is endless, people still want to work. Second, it is possible that Japanese people do not understand that they have not yet achieved a sufficient level of living standard. Although the above contradiction is interesting, we do not discuss it further in view of the fact that this is not our central concern.

Going back to the main story associated with unionization, the figure 70 per cent is too high to expect that they are interested in engaging in union activity. Leaders among non-union members have to devote much time to hearing opinions of other non-union members, to have frequent communications with other union leaders, and to persuade employers to induce their acceptance, etc. Moreover, once a union is organized with great effort, the other kind of effort such as frequent negotiations with employers and discussions with colleagues must be made to improve union members' benefit and to strengthen the power of the union. This is time-consuming physically and tiring mentally.

Finally, there is a moderate belief that unions are not effective enough to raise members' working conditions. Great effort may end in vain. Under these circumstances it is natural that few non-union members are concerned with union movement, in particular the effort to organize a new union.

We understand the implication of the answer 'Employees commit to make a sacrifice of their personal lives in exchange for hard work', as follows. Since there is such a heavy labour demand for working in the firm, employees often work overtime hours and at weekends; and sometimes, in order to accomplish their tasks within the assigned duration, do not take their paid-holidays. Occasionally, they do not mind using their private hours for inviting business partners or managers in the firm to dinners or parties.

Why do they work so hard, and accept the sacrifice of their personal lives? There are several answers to this question. First, many employees would like to receive favourable assessment from their managers as good workers in business activity in order to seek higher positions in a firm's hierarchy, as found by, for example, Tachibanaki (1998). Second, some employees simply love working and jobs, although they do not necessarily want higher positions and more wages. Third, some employees work hard in order to seek higher wages. It is necessary, nevertheless, to point out that the work ethic is now somewhat under erosion in Japan.

The first answer, namely the issue of assessment in business performance, is examined more carefully. *The Survey for Firms* which was prepared by the RIALS at the same time, namely in 1991, reports that the majority of firms have assessment systems in the business performance of each employee. Whether or not firms have an assessment system does not depend on their union status. In other words, more or less the same number of unionized and non-unionized firms have employee assessment systems.

It is reported that 40.7 per cent of non-unionized firms have a 10 per cent difference on average between the lowest and the highest figures for wage increases, which is determined by the assessment system for the business activity of each employee. The percentage figure is 30.5 per cent for the 10–20 per cent difference between the lowest and highest wage increases. These figures were comparable to Ishida (1992).

Chapter 7 of this book presents the estimated yearly earnings difference between the lowest wage earner and the highest one as 360,000 yen for 30-years-old high school graduates who work in non-unionized firms with less than 300 employees, and 400,000 yen for university graduates who have the same qualifications. This reflects largely the outcome of assessment which differentiated employees' wages, as was confirmed by Ishida (1992). In sum, wage payments are considerably different among employees, and the difference appeared due largely to the difference in assessment of individual business performance.

How do workers evaluate the assessment system in general? One question was posed as follows: is it reasonable to use the outcome of assessment in business performance for the determination of each employee's wage increase, bonus, and promotion? Over 70 per cent of respondents say 'yes', which includes both 'yes fully' and 'yes partly'. The great majority favour the use of the assessment system for the purpose of personnel management.

The next question is, 'What is the ideal wage gap between the lowest wage earner and the highest one for employees with a common age and job tenure?' Non-union members respond 'zero' wage difference with 8.4 per cent votes, 'under 20 per cent' with 26.2 per cent votes, '30–40 per cent' with 18.6 per cent votes, and 'higher than 50 per cent' with 20.0 per cent votes. This result implies that workers are fond of the principle based on free competition among employees for the determination of wages and promotion. Ishida (1992) and Chapter 7 of this book found that unions hardly interfered with this principle. In other words, unions were quite favourable towards the assessment system and its outcome. The result here signifies possible wider wage differentials among employees.

Ishida (1992) presented the fact that wages in non-unionized firms are determined more fairly than in unionized firms. 'Fairness' here includes various dimensions. (1) Wages are distributed almost equally. (2) The discrepancy between each worker's wage payment and his contribution (or marginal productivity) is very small. Since each wage earner holds his own preference for 'fairness', it is too hasty to conclude that the wage determination in non-unionized firms is fair. If many employees, nevertheless, found that wage payments were determined fairly, the role of trade unions would diminish. One of the *raisons d'être* of trade unions was to monitor industrial relations based on employees' perspective carefully, and to appeal to employers, or the third group when there is unfair treatment.

Our survey asked both union members and non-union members whether they were satisfied with employers' treatment in wages and promotion; more concretely, whether the assessment was performed fairly. The result showed, somewhat surprisingly, that the degree of dissatisfaction was higher in unionized firms than in non-unionized firms. Although it is necessary to examine the above finding more carefully by accumulating empirical studies, it reflects the fact that the assessment is performed more fairly in non-unionized firms than in unionized firms.

It would be feasible to conclude, based on the above arguments, that employees are occupied with their jobs and tasks, and thus they are not prepared to make an effort in organizing a union. The reason is that they anticipate no significant effect of a union on working conditions. They perhaps prefer to raise their wages by working harder rather than relying on the influence of a union. This reason is, probably, supported by the following observation that workers are satisfied with the current industrial relations system which does not necessarily depend on the power and influence of unions.

Let us examine whether or not the last observation is supported empirically by our data. Our hypothesis is, 'Is the degree of expectation for the role of trade unions in wage determination lower for employees who try to raise their wages on the basis of their own effort, and who believe the usefulness of the principle of competition among employees?'

We apply, again, a probit estimation procedure. The dependent variable is defined by a 0-1 dummy variable; zero signified no anticipated effect of a union on wage increase, and unity signifies some positive effect. This distinction is based on each employee's own evaluation. Although it is possible to take into consideration the effect of a union on promotion and some other variables, we consider only wage increase.

The most important independent variable is the preference of each employee about the principle of competition, i.e., wages should be determined based on employee performance in production activity. Scaling of this variable was made in the following way: the numerical figure 1 is given to the preference that all employees should receive equal wages, if their ages and educational attainments are common; 2 is given to the case in which the difference between the highest earner and the lowest one should be kept within 20 per cent; 3 is given to the case between 20 per cent and 30 per cent; 4 is given to the case over 50 per cent; and 5 is given to the case in which no regulation on wage determination should be provided. The other independent variables such as sex, age, job tenure, occupation, industry, firm size, and the degree of satisfaction with wages are added.

Table 3.6 shows the estimated result for all non-union employees, equation (1), and male white-collar non-union employees, equation (2), respectively. The most valuable observation in both equations (1) and (2) is that the estimated coefficient for the preference of competition is negative with statistical significance, implying that employees who prefer the competition system based on employee performance have a lower degree of expectation for the role of unions in wage determination. We are able to support our hypothesis that employees who do not mind working hard, or make an effort in job tasks, are not interested in the effect or the role of unions.

Several comments are made on the estimated coefficients of the other independent variables. First, since the sex coefficient is positive

Table 3.6 The expectation for anticipated effect of unions (%)

	Equation (1)	*Equation (2)*
Preference for competition principle based on employee performance	−0.082*	−0.135**
	(1.906)	(2.199)
Sex (male; 1, female; zero)	0.244**	
	(1.726)	
Age	0.058	0.009
	(0.716)	(0.699)
Education	−0.088	0.080**
	(0.267)	(1.976)
Job tenure	0.017	−0.014
	(0.149)	(0.954)
Satisfaction with wages	−0.102	−0.240**
	(1.690)	(2.516)
Log-likelihood	−394.14	−208.74

Notes: (1) Figures in parentheses are estimated asymptotic *t*-values.
(2) Equation (1) is estimated for all employees, and equation (2) is for male white-collar employees. Coefficients for industry dummy, occupational dummy and firm size are not written in this table.
(3) Figures in parentheses are estimated coefficients over standard errors.
(4) * implies statistical significance at the 0.1 level, and ** at the 0.05 level.

with statistical significance, female expectation for trade unions is lower than the male one. This confirms the previous result regarding the difference in attitude towards unions between men and women. Second, the negative coefficient of satisfaction with wages implies 'The higher the satisfaction level, the lower the expectation for unions.' Third, the number of statistically significant coefficients in equation (2) is larger than that in equation (1), indicating that male white-collar workers are, in general, more negative on the role of unions. In particular, those who have higher educational attainments are quite negative concerning the effectiveness of unions.

The probit analysis confirmed our hypothesis statistically: employees who are positive for the role of competition based on personal performance in wage determination are more negative about the role of unions. Since the current industrial relations system in Japan moves towards this direction, it is possible to anticipate that the degree of expectation for trade unions will diminish gradually. Of course, the aspect of wages is not the only factor which is affected by the union power. Therefore, it is too early to conclude that the role of unions will diminish. The other conditions regarding the role of unions must be taken into account in order to reach the final conclusion. The most important factor, nevertheless, is wages for employees. Thus, our tentative conclusion will not be modified even if we take into consideration aspects other than wages.

The analysis of this part leads us to the following summary. Non-union members say that there are not many workers who are interested in organizing a union, and in becoming a leader. Many non-union members take the view that 'it is not me but somebody else who should take an initiative'. They prefer hard-working to raise their promotion possibility and wages rather than spending their time in taking the trouble to organize a union, or to become a union leader. In other words, they wish to be recognized by the firm as productive workers rather than by their colleagues as workers who have strong solidarity. Simply speaking, many employees are fond of individualism rather than collectivism. In terms of economics it is possible to state that the preference for job tasks is higher than that for time for union activity in workers' minds.

Trade unions, traditionally, had the principle of egalitarianism among union members, and thus did not accept the industrial relations system which produces wider wage differentials among them. This was true in many countries in the world. For example, see Sano (1969) for Japan, and Freeman (1982) for the US. Our finding obtained here gives us one counter-example against the tradition. We do not proclaim that the change in the attitude of employees described here is common in all unions. We merely say that it is only an increasing trend. This is, in particular, true among unions in the highly competitive industries whose employees are largely white-collar workers. One example is the Electric Industry Union which abandoned recently the principle of egalitarianism (i.e., the seniority rule for the determination of promotion and wages).

One policy option for trade unions under these circumstances is to change their principle from supporting the seniority system to supporting the competition system. One important role of trade unions is to monitor whether the competition system works efficiently and fairly. If members of trade unions find that the system works unfairly, they can protest to employers and demand a change in the assessment system. In sum, the contribution of trade unions can be large, if they support the system in a practical manner.

3.6 Concluding remarks

This chapter examined and discussed the view of non-union members on unions, the attitude of employees on the principle of competition based on personal performance, and the expectation for unions.

We provide a brief summary of the findings: the barriers against organizing a union are described as follows. First, the lack of leaders who take an initiative is serious, as many non-union members point out. It is difficult to expect non-union members who are quite busy with jobs and tasks in the firm to raise their hands. It is time to contemplate a method which is able to provide a possible leader with incentives.

Second, we found that some groups of employees, namely females, white-collar workers, and employees in the non-manufacturing industries, understood that the effect of a union on various working conditions including wages was very marginal. Since the proportion of these groups of employees in the total labour force is increasing, it is difficult to imagine that a strong desire for a new union will be held among non-union members, even if a motivated leader appeals, or a strong outside pressure appears.

Third, we pointed out that a large number of workers are too busy to become leaders to organize a union. Moreover, they want to work hard to seek higher positions in the firm's hierarchy, and then higher wages, rather than relying on the influence of a union for an increase in wages. This may be, in fact, the most serious obstacle against union movement in general. We described several policies to overcome this obstacle, by raising several alternative methods.

Another important area in which unions can greatly contribute is in their safety-net role in the event of discharges and layoffs, according to our judgement. The recent serious recession forced many firms in Japan to adopt a strict restructuring policy unfortunately, including a large number of discharges and layoffs. The problem of discharges and layoffs was not the major issue in the past thanks to the fairly prosperous Japanese economy. The recent recession stopped the guarantee of a permanent employment system in a substantial number of firms.

It is impossible, of course, to avoid all discharges and layoffs, since economically rational decisions by firms, which force firms to have some discharges and layoffs unavoidably, can be accepted from the macro and national economic point of view. Discharges and layoffs can contribute to keeping the loss of resources and welfare to a minimum. We observe, however, a limited number of unlawful and economically unjustified discharges and layoffs. Trade unions are expected to react to these events strongly in order to prevent such discharges and layoffs from being allowed. This is a safety-net role of unions. Union members will feel the necessity of a union if such actions are successful.

4
Union Voice, and Its Effect on Satisfaction and Separation

4.1 Introduction

Satisfaction of workers plays an important role in the determination of workers' behaviour such as labour turnover, work incentive, etc. Freeman and Medoff (1984), and Freeman (1980a), for example, investigated the role of satisfaction in the determination of separations from firms, and obtained the fact that satisfied workers tend to stay in the firm. Also, they investigated the role of union-voice when unions (or employees) want to transmit their members' feelings and opinions to employers. They found that strong union-voices against employers reduced the degree of dissatisfaction among union members because employers listened to these voices and modified their management policy to deal with employees' dissatisfaction.

The above description suggests the importance of satisfaction (or dissatisfaction) variables of employees in the determination of labour turnover and in the domain of industrial relations in general. The purpose of this chapter is to investigate the role of the variable of satisfaction of employees explicitly. The reason why we investigate it is that this variable, namely satisfaction, has not been used explicitly in empirical studies, but has been used only conceptually. In other words, the degree of each worker's satisfaction has not been investigated, although it played a role only in the conceptual sense to predict the actual behaviour of each employee. There are several examples in Japan, nevertheless, which paid attention to this variable, such as Lincoln and Kalleberg (1990), Tsuru, Hayashi and Rebitzer (1993), and Ishikawa (1996). They used the information on workers' satisfaction level, and investigated the role of it in labour turnover and job effort. Tsuru, Hayashi and Rebitzer conclude that although unions had prepared a channel for raising their voice, the channel was unable to raise the degree of employees' satisfaction, and thus to reduce the extent of labour turnover. They attribute the lack of success in stopping the lowering of the union participation rate in Japan to unions' failure in guranteeing the above channel.

The studies by Freeman and Medoff (1984), Freeman (1980a) and Tsuru *et al.* (1993) suggest to us the following implication: when we investigate the effect of satisfaction on labour turnover, it is important to recognize that there are two conflicting channels or cases on the effect. The first is that some satisfied workers do not stay in the firm, but try to change their employers to seek better employers. In this case, the distinction between unionized workers and non-unionized workers does not matter at all because workers change their employers in any case. Of course, the remaining part of satisfied workers would remain in the firm because they are *satisfied*. It is natural to anticipate that unsatisfied workers would leave the firm, when there are no unions who listen to their dissatisfaction. The second is that unsatisfied workers, in fact, do not change their employers, but stay in the firm. The second case supposes that dissatisfaction expressed by employees is handled by unions adequately, and then it is transmitted to the management side as a voice. Both unions and employers take various actions in various fields of daily job and task activities to reduce the degree of dissatisfaction and to improve working conditions, and thus employees stay in the firm finally.

These two cases suggest that it is too simplistic to believe that all unsatisfied workers in unionized firms will leave the firm. Some unsatisfied workers would stay if their dissatisfaction were listened to carefully and handled well by unions and employers. Of course, some other unsatisfied workers would leave despite possible better treatment by unions and employers. The story for employees in non-unionized firms is that the rate of separations for unsatisfied workers in those firms will be higher because the absence of unions excludes significant capability of a better treatment, if we believe the effect of union-voices. Union-voices here signify that the above better treatment for unsatisfied workers initiated by unions and followed by employers works well.

It is possible to conceive of the following hypothesis, after we discussed the relationship between satisfaction and unions: there are two kinds of dissatisfaction among employees. The first is dissatisfaction which could be handled by both unions and employers through the mechanism of union-voices, and the second is dissatisfaction which could not be handled by them, and which would thus lead workers to leave the firm eventually. The first may be called fictitious, controllable or can-be-handled dissatisfaction, while the second may be called intrinsic dissatisfaction.

It would be interesting to find out which working and labour condition belongs to the first among various working and labour conditions such as working hours, wages, job assignments, etc, and which one belongs to the second. Another interesting subject is to find whether or not there is any difference between unionized firms and non-unionized firms regarding the relative significance between the first and the second kind of dissatisfaction. In other words, do employees in unionized firms tend to express the first kind of dissatisfaction more apparently and significantly than those in non-unionized firms? How about the second kind? Finally, it would be interesting to inquire into the following question: is there any difference between the first and second dissatisfactions regarding the effect on actual labour turnover? We would like to investigate these questions by applying a fruitful data source.

4.2 Empirical results

The data source is the Rengo's *Survey on Jobs and Working Condition* in 1991. The most important feature of this survey is that it includes employees in both unionized firms and non-unionized firms. Thus, we are able to draw the difference between the influence of the existence of unions and that of the absence of unions regarding the satisfaction level and motivation of employees.

The first subject which we investigate is the feeling of employees on their working conditions and environment. In particular, we examine the degree of propensity to leave (and to stay) among employees who are separated by the different degree of satisfaction of employees with respect to their working conditions. Simply, we would like to know whether or not satisfied workers wish to stay in the firm more strongly than dissatisfied workers.

The particular question in the survey asks, 'How do you evaluate a change in employers (i.e., separation from one firm to another firm)?' Four answers were prepared for this question. First, I do not have any intention to leave the firm because I am satisfied with the current firm. Second, I would not change the firm unless the working conditions, including wage payments, in other firms would be higher by more than 20 per cent than that in the current firm, provided that the job assignment or content is the same as the current one. Third, I would like to move to another firm because the job assignment and working conditions in the current firm are unsatisfactory, even if the wage level in another firm would be the same as the one in the current firm. Fourth, I would like to move to another firm when the job assignment at another firm is appealing and thus satisfactory for me, even if the other working conditions would be somewhat inferior. We regard the first two answers as employees who have high 'propensity to stay', and the last two answers as those who have high 'propensity to move'. We call them stayers and movers, respectively, for the sake of simplicity. We examine male employees only here.

Table 4.1 shows the proportion of stayers and that of movers for each separated item of working conditions, and for unionized firms and non-unionized firms, respectively. We pay attention to the difference between satisfied workers and dissatisfied ones. We, first, examine the case of unionized firms. Among dissatisfied workers with the current job assignment (i.e., nature, quality and character of job), 52.54 per cent of employees in unionized firms are movers, while 28.81 per cent are stayers. Among satisfied workers with the current job assignment only 15 per cent of employees in unionized firms are movers. The above result suggests that there appears to be significant difference between satisfied workers and dissatisfied workers regarding the degree of propensity to move. Simply, satisfied workers have much stronger propensity to stay than dissatisfied workers. When we pay attention to the effect of easiness of job, we find that 46 per cent of dissatisfied employees are movers and 36 per cent are stayers, while only

Table 4.1 Proportions of employees who show propensity to move. Employees are separated by their satisfaction level (%)

	Unionized firms	*Non-unionized firms*
Wages		
High	26.67	35.29
Low	30.40	34.75
Working hours		
Short	38.46	55.56
Long	35.71	32.23
Job assignment		
Satisfied	15.00	14.81
Dissatisfied	52.54	62.71
Easiness of job		
Satisfied	16.89	18.52
Dissatisfied	46.00	48.00

16.89 per cent of satisfied employees are movers. A similar story was obtained between the effect of job assignment (i.e., quality of job) and that of easiness of job.

The effect of wages suggests that the influence of wages gives a much smaller difference between satisfied workers (i.e., employees who report that they receive higher wages) and dissatisfied workers (i.e., employees who report that they receive lower wages) in the determination of movers and stayers than the influence of job assignment and/or easiness of job. It is, nevertheless, true that employees who report that they receive lower wages have a still higher propensity to move. The overall observation in Table 4.1 concludes that employees who are unsatisfied with various working conditions have a strong propensity to move.

Next, we examine the case of employees in non-unionized firms in Table 4.1. Among employees who are dissatisfied with job assignment 62.71 per cent desire to move, while only 14.81 per cent of satisfied employees desire to move. This is the significant difference. A similar difference is observed also for the easiness of job between dissatisfied workers, i.e., 48 per cent and satisfied workers, i.e., 18.52 per cent. The difference with respect to wages, however, is very marginal, although the degree of propensity to move among satisfied workers with current wages is somewhat higher than that among dissatisfied workers.

All the observations described above give us the following conclusion: when the degree of satisfaction with various working conditions, in particular those associated with job quality and easiness, is lower, the propensity to move is stronger. This conclusion is applicable for employees in both unionized and non-unionized firms. More concretely speaking, the proportion of employees whose propensity to move is strong among dissatisfied employees, and the proportion of employees whose propensity to move is also strong among satisfied employees are considerably different, when we are concerned with the effect of various working conditions, in particular job quality and easiness. It implies that the probability of leaving the firm is higher for dissatisfied workers (i.e., those who feel a negative evaluation on working conditions) than for satisfied workers (i.e., those who feel a positive evaluation). This suggests that the data support the view that the second kind of dissatisfaction defined previously is more realistic and plausible than the first kind, provided that dissatisfaction has an influence on the determination for the actual degree of separations of employees from the firm.

Therefore, it is possible to predict that unions will affect the degree of employees' satisfaction positively under the assumption that unions have some voice. In other words, the following equations would be possible:

$$\begin{cases} S = S(U, X) \\ \partial S/\partial U > 0 \end{cases}$$

where S is the degree of satisfaction, U is the union dummy, and X is the independent personal characteristics. We are going to examine whether or not data support the above equations.

4.3 Simple statistical test

Before investigating the data in detail, a simple statistical test is attempted to examine whether there is a difference between employees in unionized firms and those in non-unionized firms regarding employees' satisfaction level. Table 4.2 shows some statistics (i.e., t-test) for employees whose ages are 34-years-old and younger. These statistics were calculated under the assumption that the numerical value 4 was assigned to the highest satisfaction level, and 0 was assigned to the lowest satisfaction level. Of course, the numbers 3, 2 and 1 are also used to represent the intermediary level of satisfaction.

When we pay attention to the two items of working conditions, namely wages and job assignments (i.e., characters), the degree of satisfaction of employees in unionized firms is higher than that in non-unionized firms. The difference is not statistically significant at the 5 per cent level, while it is statistically significant at the 10 per cent level. The item of easiness of job supports the 5 per cent statistical significance for the difference. As for both working hours and assessment in job performance made by superior persons in the hierarchical ladder, the satisfaction level is higher among employees in unionized firms than those in non-unionized firms, although it is not statistically significant. A similar situation is observed also for the degree of staying in the firm. The only exception is the item of fairness of assessment in employee job performance because employees in non-unionized firms are more satisfied than those in unionized firms at the 5 per cent level.

The overall result based on a simple statistical test in Table 4.2 provides us with the following conclusion: there is no significant difference between workers in unionized firms and those in non-unionized firms regarding the degree of workers' satisfaction level, although the satisfaction in the former is marginally higher than the satisfaction in the latter. It is important to supplement the fact that the empirical result in Table 4.2 has been obtained without controlling for the

Table 4.2 Statistical test of the degree of satisfaction between employees in unionized firms and those in non-unionized firms

	Unionized firms		*Non-unionized firms*		
	Average	*Standard deviation*	*Average*	*Standard deviation*	t-*value*
Wages	1.482	0.794	1.343	0.893	−1.938
Working hours	1.467	0.923	1.441	0.932	−0.332
Job assignment	2.492	1.129	2.324	1.102	−1.771
Easiness of job	2.407	1.025	2.095	1.038	−3.552
Fair assessment for employee performance	1.752	1.042	1.959	1.045	2.333
Evaluation of superior persons in hierarchical ladder	2.125	1.061	2.003	1.124	−1.305
Propensity to stay in the firm	2.311	1.364	2.169	1.430	−1.197

Note: The number of observations is 598.

influence of other variables which are supposed to affect workers' satisfaction level possibly. Thus, it is necessary to take into consideration some possible effect of these control variables. The next task is such an attempt.

4.4 The union's effect on the level of workers' satisfaction

This section presents the empirical result which was estimated by an ordered probit model, after controlling for the effect of various variables. The control is made by introducing many variables into the following regression equation as the independent variables.

$$Y_i = \beta_0 + \beta_1\, Age_i + \beta_2\, Tenure_i + \beta_3\, Education_i$$
$$+ \beta_4\, Profession_i + \beta_5\, Size_i + \beta_6\, Union_i + \beta_7\, Others_i + U_i$$

where *Age* is employee's age, *Tenure* is his job tenure in the firm, *Education* is a dummy variable (junior college and college graduates, 1, otherwise, 0), *Profession* is a dummy variable for his occupation (white-collar, 1, otherwise, 0), *Size* is the natural log of the number of employees in the firm), *Union* is a dummy variable (unionized firm, 1, non-unionized, 0), and *Others* is several other variables. U_i is a random term.

Y_i is the degree of *i*-th employee satisfaction which is defined as follows,

$Y_i < 0$	unsatisfied
$0 \leqq Y_i < \alpha_1$	somewhat unsatisfied
$\alpha_1 \leqq Y_i < \alpha_2$	indifferent
$\alpha_2 \leqq Y_i < \alpha_3$	somewhat satisfied
$\alpha_3 \leqq Y_i$	satisfied

where 0, α_1, α_2, and α_3 are threshold parameters which are supposed to show the degree of satisfaction as indicated above. We estimate both parameters like β_i ($i = 1, \ldots, 7$) and thresholds like α_i ($i = 1, 2, 3$) by a maximum likelihood method. Tables 4.3 and 4.4 show the empirical results.

Our first concern is to examine whether or not the existence of a union has an effect on the determination of employees' satisfaction. We described previously our hypothesis, namely, if a union had a stronger voice than a non-union, a union would have a positive effect on satisfaction. Such a hypothesis can be tested by seeing the sign of the estimated coefficient of the union dummy variable.

It would be necessary to explain how data were quantified. As for the satisfaction of each item, it was explained before; the highest

Table 4.3 The effect of the voices on labour conditions and work environment (male)

	Job assignment	*Easiness of job*	*Wage*	*Working hours*	*Assessment on employee performance*
Firm size	0.035	0.046	0.000	−0.080	0.095**
	(0.733)	(1.061)	(0.004)	(1.571)	(2.147)
Satisfaction with wages	0.119*			0.260**	0.228**
	(1.894)			(4.908)	(3.929)
Log wages			0.668**		
			(3.454)		
Satisfaction with assessment on employee performance	0.174**		0.299**		
	(3.620)		(6.185)		
Sacrifice in personal life	0.127**		−0.074*	−0.384**	
	(3.285)		(1.821)	(9.126)	
Easiness of job	0.554**				
	(10.27)				
Manager's assessment	0.133**	0.460**			0.386**
	(2.330)	(9.014)			(7.779)
Job assessment	0.274**	0.264**			
	(4.623)	(5.189)			
Union dummy	−0.580	0.000	0.465	0.820**	−0.769**
	(1.354)	(0.002)	(1.367)	(2.009)	(1.961)
log-likelihood	−640.03	−667.09	−603.32	−621.80	−697.94

Notes: Figures in upper-part are estimated coefficients, and those in parentheses are asymptotic *t*-values. The number of observations is 598. *Statistically significant at the 0.1 level, and ** at the 0.05 level. The coefficients on job tenure, age, education and industry dummies are not written in this table because of their statistical insignificance.

Table 4.4 The effect of the voices on labour conditions and work environment (female)

	Job assignment	*Easiness of job*	*Wage*	*Working hours*
Firm size	0.027	−0.014**	−0.175**	−0.166**
	(0.503)	(0.207)	(3.094)	(3.087)
Satisfaction with wages	0.139*			0.285**
	(1.822)			(4.214)
Log wages			−0.074	
			(0.399)	
Satisfaction with assessment on employee performance	0.095		0.248**	
	(1.449)		(3.902)	
Sacrifice in personal life	0.193**		−0.001	−0.219**
	(4.064)		(0.024)	(4.802)
Easiness of job	0.504**			
	(7.085)			
Manager's assessment	0.185**	0.421**		
	(2.690)	(6.714)		
Job assessment	0.176**	0.311**		
	(2.568)	(4.738)		
Union dummy	−0.401	−0.031	0.098	−0.477*
	(1.178)	(0.086)	(0.863)	(1.863)
Log-likelihood	−417.59	−368.85	−404.00	−354.66

Notes: Figures in upper-part are estimated coefficients, and those in parentheses are asymptotic *t*-values. The number of observations is 395. *Statistically significant at the 0.1 level, and ** at the 0.05 level. The coefficients on job tenure, age, education and industry dummies are not written in this table because of their statistical insignificance.

satisfaction is equal to 5, and the lowest one is equal to 1. For example, the highest satisfaction regarding job assignment is 5, somewhat satisfied is 4, indifferent is 3, somewhat dissatisfied is 2, and unsatisfied is 1. The similar quantification was made for easiness of job, working hours, and superior persons (i.e., managerial persons) in the hierarchical ladder, respectively. As for job procedure, 'the highest consensus is required' is 5, and 'the lowest consensus is required' is 1. This variable is concerned with the degree of consensus among employees to achieve a goal. As for fairness of assessment of employee job performance, the highest fairness is 5, and the highest unfairness is 1. As for sacrifice of personal life, the highest sacrifice is 5, and the lowest one is 1. In sum, all variables are quantified by 5, 4, 3, 2, and 1.

The result for male observations is examined first. Table 4.3 is the estimated result. The union dummy is not statistically significant to explain the satisfaction of job assignment. The variables which explain (i.e., affect) it are the satisfaction of easiness of job, of job procedure, and of fairness of assessment for employee performance. A similar result was obtained by Muramatsu (1993) for the same data source as this study, although the estimation method is considerably different. The union dummy variable is not statistically significant to explain easiness of job, either.

As for the satisfaction of both wages and working hours, we find statistical insignificance of the union dummy variable for wages, although the estimated coefficient is positive. The union dummy is positive with statistical significance for working hours. These results suggest that workers in unionized firms are more satisfied with working hours than those in non-unionized firms, although there is no significant difference between them regarding the satisfaction of wages. It is consistent with the finding by Tachibanaki and Noda (1993) who proposed that there was no significant difference in wage payments between unionized firms and non-unionized firms, and that there appeared some positive union effect on regular working hours. Finally, it is noted that the union dummy is negative with statistical significance for fairness of assessment for employee performance, indicating that workers in unionized firms are unsatisfied with assessment in employee job performance by employers.

Next, female observations are examined. It is reported in Table 4.4. The union dummy variable is not statistically significant for both job assignment and easiness of job. It is not statistically significant for wages like the case of male observations, but the sign is negative for working hours unlike the case of male observations. The latter finding suggests that female workers in unionized firms are dissatisfied with working hours.

The overall result leads to the conclusion that the only item which can be affected by unions rigorously is working hours for male workers, among various working conditions which unions are supposed to affect through their voices. Moreover, male employees in unionized firms are, in fact, more unsatisfied with respect to fairness of assessment for employee performance than those in non-unionized firms. A similar story holds for female employees regarding the satisfaction of working hours. As for both job assignment and easiness of job, unions are unlikely to increase the satisfaction level of both male and female employees. In sum, unions are only effective for raising the satisfaction level of working hours for male employees, and are not effective for the other items at all.

Tsuru, Hayashi and Rebitzer (1993) obtained the fact that unions had no effect on the increase in the satisfaction level of general working conditions. Our result confirms it, by showing that many detailed items such as wages, working hours, job assignment, assessment in employee job performance etc. have the similar result. Unions do not have any significant positive effect on the increase in the satisfaction level about many different kinds of working conditions (i.e., items). Does this finding have any effect for labour turnover? In other words, does our finding have any implications for the story of labour turnover? This is the next issue.

4.5 The effect of union voices on labour turnover

This part investigates the effect of both unions and the level of satisfaction on labour turnover, and examines whether or not unions are able to reduce the rate of separations from the firm through a positive effect on satisfaction of employees. If workers in unionized firms can recognize the role of unions, which raise their satisfaction or reduce their dissatisfaction, they are more likely to stay in their firm than those in non-unionized firms. We apply, again, an ordered probit model for the above purpose.

Table 4.5 shows the estimated result for the equation of the degree of staying in the firm. The dependent variable, namely, propensity to stay, is measured by the question, 'How do you evaluate a change in employers?' which was used previously. The quantification method is the same as the previous one. The independent variables are a union dummy, size of firm, some other control variables and various items of the satisfaction variables which were used in the previous tables. The staying function and the satisfaction variables form a kind of reduced form equations.

We, first, examine male observations. Equation (1) includes only the union dummy variable and several control variables in the independent variables, while equation (2) adds various items of satisfaction variables to those in equation (1). We find that the union dummy is not statistically significant in the two equations, although it shows the positive coefficients. We can say that unions have no effect on propensity to stay. The effect of each item of satisfaction, i.e., job assignment and easiness of job, fairness of assessment for employee performance, and working hours, has the positive effect with statistical significance on propensity to stay. These results suggest the following conclusion; when we compare the influence of unions and the

Table 4.5 The effect of the voices on the retention rates

	Male		*Female*	
	(1)	*(2)*	*(1)*	*(2)*
Firm size	0.071	0.000	0.051	0.031
	(1.635)	(0.019)	(1.425)	(0.601)
Satisfaction with wages		0.088		0.076
		(1.312)		(1.062)
Satisfaction with working hours		0.104*		0.120
		(1.788)		(0.145)
Satisfaction with assessment on employee performance		0.113**		0.052
		(2.091)		(0.760)
Sacrifice in personal life		0.012**		−0.142**
		(0.268)		(2.653)
Job assignment		0.368**		0.291**
		(6.448)		(4.466)
Easiness of job		0.137**		0.311**
		(2.253)		(3.859)
Union dummy	0.120	0.165	0.008	0.018
	(0.329)	(0.386)	(0.425)	(0.065)
Log-likelihood	−667.09	−690.35	−650.87	−688.34

Notes: Figures in upper-part are estimated coefficients, and those in parentheses are asymptotic t-values. The number of male observations is 598. The number of female observations is 395. *Statistically significant at the 0.1 level, and ** at the 0.05 level. The coefficients on job tenure, age, education and industry dummies are not written in this table because of their statistical insignificance.

satisfaction of employees, the latter is much stronger than the former for the determination of propensity to stay for workers. At the same time, if the degree of propensity to stay were different among workers, the difference in each item of satisfaction would be responsible.

Next, we examine female observations. Since the union dummy variable is not statistically significant, a union does not affect propensity to stay for female workers like male workers. Both wages and working hours are not statistically significant; propensity to stay is not influenced by these satisfaction levels. Fairness of assessment for employee performance has no effect on propensity to stay, unlike the case of male workers. Satisfaction associated with job assignment and easiness of job has a positive effect on propensity to stay, like the case of male workers. An interesting contrast appears between men and women when we examine the effect of personal life satisfaction; while it has no effect on propensity to stay for males, it has a negative effect for females, suggesting that if females feel that they sacrifice their personal life, they have lower propensity to stay. The overall result for females, nevertheless, suggests that the effect of satisfaction associated with job on propensity to stay is stronger than that associated with working conditions.

By combining the empirical result for males and females estimated by the ordered probit model, it can be concluded that unions do not play an important role, and thus there is no difference in the determination of propensity to stay between unionized firms and non-unionized firms. The variables which affect propensity to stay for males are the satisfactions of job assignment, easiness of job, fairness of assessment for employee performance and working hours, and for females are those of job assignment and easiness of job. In general, satisfaction associated with job and fair assessment for employee performance is more important than satisfaction associated with wages and working hours. Tomita (1993) suggested a similar possibility. We confirm, based on the econometric study, that his conjecture was right. Tomita's and our results have an important implication for unions, because the two studies recommend that unions should take care of their members' problems which are related to jobs and fair assessment for performance rather than the traditional working conditions such as wages and working hours. These issues are crucial for the determination of the satisfaction level of workers, who are concerned more with their jobs and tasks rather than with wages and working hours.

Among variables which have some influence on propensity to stay for males is satisfaction associated with working hours and fair assessment for employee performance. For the former (i.e., working hours) a union has a positive effect, while it has a negative effect for the latter. Other variables do not have any effect by unions for both males and females. Therefore, it can be concluded that unions have no strong effect to increase workers' propensity to stay. This is consistent with the conclusion given by Tsuru, Hayashi and Rebitzer (1993) who proposed that unions were unsuccessful in lowering dissatisfaction of employees in unionized firms, and thus in lowering propensity to stay.

The last conclusion should be evaluated carefully because it is inconsistent with the general impression held in Japan that unions have some positive effect in lowering the degree of separations from the firm, as given by, for example, Tomita (1993) and the subsequent chapters in this book.

There are several crucial points which can explain the cause of such an apparent inconsistency. First, it is important to recognize that the principal concern in this chapter is employees' *propensity* to stay, but not employees' *actual* stay or separation. In other words, workers express only their preference or opinions on labour turnover, and they do not indicate their real actions of labour turnover. It is quite natural that preference (i.e., opinion) and action are separated in human behaviour. In other words, expectation and outcome are different. Thus, it is possible that the case based on the former and the case based on the latter are different. Obviously, we have analyzed this chapter based on the former.

Second, our study uses the satisfaction variable as an explicit intermediary indicator which transmits from workers' qualifications to propensity to stay in the firm. At the same time, we consider a large number of different items in the satisfaction variables such as job assignment, working hours, etc. There are, in principle, two different stages which transmit from workers' qualifications to propensity to stay. The first is from workers' qualifications to satisfaction, and the second is from satisfaction to propensity to stay. Since this study did not investigate the relative weight between the first stage and the second stage in interpreting the total effect (i.e., entire story), it is impossible to identify which stage is more crucial. Consequently, it is possible to misunderstand whether the first stage or the second stage dominated the whole story.

Third, it is possible to guess that there are a small number of workers who are highly dissatisfied with the current working conditions and environment, but never leave the firm. On the other hand, there are a small number of workers who are highly satisfied, but leave the firm easily. The existence of these two extreme workers is likely to make the relationship among unions, satisfaction and labour turnover more complicated, even if the number of these workers is small.

In sum, we can conclude that we do not find any significant inconsistency between our result and the other studies for the reasons described above.

4.6 Concluding remarks

This chapter investigated the influence of unions on workers' propensity to stay (i.e., preference) with explicit consideration of the satisfaction level in their working life. We obtained the following conclusions.

First, there are two different kinds of dissatisfaction. The first is controllable, and the second is intrinsic. The difference between the two is crucial for the determination of employees' separation from the firm.

The first does not affect separation, while the second may affect it. When we examined various satisfaction variables, it was found that dissatisfaction among Japanese employees was intrinsic. In particular, dissatisfaction associated with jobs and tasks was intrinsic. At the same time, such an intrinsic satisfaction lowered the degree of propensity to stay (i.e., preference) in the firm.

Second, we examined whether or not unions had a voice effect on raising workers' satisfaction, by applying an ordered probit model to individual observations data. It was found that although unions had a positive effect on satisfaction associated with working hours for male workers, they had no effect on satisfaction associated with job assignment, easiness of job, superior persons in the hierarchical ladder, and wages. Incidentally, workers in unionized firms are more dissatisfied with fair assessment for employee performance than those in non-unionized firms. For female workers, employees in unionized firms are more dissatisfied with working hours than those in non-unionized firms. A similar story holds for the other items of satisfaction variables between female workers and male workers. These results imply that unions did not have any strong voice effect which increased the degree of workers' satisfaction.

Third, we examined whether unions raised employees' propensity to stay in the firm by reducing the dissatisfaction level in many items. It was found that the higher the satisfaction level in job assignment, easiness of job, fair assessment for employee performance, and working hours, the higher the propensity to stay in the firm. Since it was found previously that unions did not contribute to raising the satisfaction level in these various items except for male working hours, it could be concluded that unions were not successful in increasing workers' propensity to stay (i.e., preference) in the firm. The third point is inconsistent with the common understanding with respect to the role of unions in Japan. The previous section described several clues to explain that it is not, in fact, inconsistent.

5
The Effect of Unions on Wages

5.1 Introduction

It is a fairly popular subject in the UK and the US to inquire into the quantitative effect of the union/non-union wage differentials. In particular, the number of empirical studies on the effect of trade unions in the US is impressively large, as shown by the number of references given in several survey articles and books such as Lewis (1986), Addison and Hirsch (1989), Booth (1995), etc. The number of studies in Japan, however, is very limited in both quantity and quality.

Why are there so many studies in the US while there are few studies in Japan? First, there is a large amount of data in the US, especially individual workers' data, which include information on wages, individual workers' qualifications and, of course, the union status of each worker. Information on each worker's union status has not been easily available in Japan, although excellent data on wages and related information are available given, representatively, by the *Wage Structure Survey* published by the Ministry of Labour. *Excellent* means that the number of observations in this data source is over one million, and that several important variables on individual workers and firms are available. Nearly all studies for wages have used this data source in Japan. Individual observations on wages, however, are not easily available for public use, unfortunately.

Second, the difference in the number of empirical-oriented economists, in particular labour economists, between the US and Japan is enormous. Labour economics, in particular economics of trade unions, has not been a popular subject in Japan for various reasons.

Third, there has been a common understanding in the US that there remains a significant positive effect of trade unions on wage premium. Thus, it makes sense for economists to investigate how significant the quantitative effect of trade unions on wages is. There has been an implicit understanding in Japan, despite the lack of studies, that there is no union/non-union wage differential. Therefore, there is no strong incentive among Japanese economists to perform a study which estimates the union effect. We believe, in fact, that the third reason is the most important, at least for Japan.

We, both researchers and institutions (namely, the RIALS), made an effort to build our own data, by committing to conduct two surveys which include useful information on union status, wages, various working conditions, workers' own assessments about various matters, and on firms, to fill a gap in data availability.

The research strategy to find the effect of trade unions on wages is as follows. First, we estimate parameters of wage functions for employees in both unionized firms and non-unionized firms, and then we calculate the quantitative difference in wages between unionized firms and non-unionized firms based on the estimated parameters.

There remain, however, several technical problems such as a simultaneous equation problem and a sample selection bias in the estimation of pure union/non-union wage differentials. These problems are solved later in this book. The purpose of this chapter is to present merely an intuitively appealing result of union/non-union wage differentials based on a relatively easy method.

There are two approaches when we estimate the effect of trade unions on wages. The first approach is to investigate whether or not there are differences in various dimensions of business performances between a firm with a trade union and a firm without a trade union provided that the other conditions are common between them. The second approach is to estimate the difference in wage payments between a union member and a non-union member.

These two approaches are, in fact, identical, at least in Japan, because trade unions in Japan can be characterized by enterprise unionism, and at the same time they are, in principle, closed-shops, as was explained previously. In other words, if we estimate wage differentials between employees in unionized firms and those in non-unionized firms, we are able to achieve the above two approaches simultaneously because of enterprise unionism and closed-shops. A similar strategy is applicable for the effect of unions on working conditions of employees, productivity in firms, etc. In sum, it is necessary and sufficient to compare unionized firms and non-unionized firms, at least in Japan, in order to draw the difference in many variables like wages between union members and non-union members.

The determination of wages is influenced by a large number of factors such as employees' personal characteristics, firms' economic conditions, as well as union status. It is important to control for the contribution of these factors in order to reveal a pure union/non-union wage differential. Therefore, it would be useful to recognize empirically how these factors affect the determination of wages in Japan. The next section gives a brief introduction to literature in Japan, which will help readers to understand the subsequent analysis more easily.

5.2 A brief introduction to wage determination in Japan

Since the determination of wages is affected by a large number of factors including the contribution of trade unions, it is useful to recognize the empirical story of those factors in order to understand the pure effect of unions on wages more easily. This part depends largely on Tachibanaki (1996a) who discussed the wage determination in Japan comprehensively, and we summarize its conclusions very briefly.

(1) The male/female difference is the most significant determinant, and its main cause is discrimination against women. This result is observed when both males and females are included in the sample. In particular, it appears for raw data which have not been adjusted for any weights of demographic factors or qualifications. In other words, simple nominal wage figures, with no adjustment for other qualifications such as job tenure, education, or occupation, which pertain to both males and females, suggest that gender is the most influential among many factors in wage differentials.

It is worthwhile to attempt to discover what happens if other qualifications are common between males and females. It is possible, for example, to insist that the average job tenure of females is shorter than males because of obvious and occasional interruptions of working activities peculiar to females. Under the seniority payment system in Japan, women would receive lower wage payments than men because of their shorter job tenures.

It is proposed that the difference in qualifications between males and females such as job tenure, education, etc. are not responsible for wider wage differentials between males and females. The most important element is the differential *treatment* of worker qualifications between males and females in the determination of their wages. This is discrimination. Discrimination against women is rooted in contemporary Japanese industrial relations. Every country in the world has such a tendency; its degree in Japan, however, is higher than in other countries by international standards.

(2) Education, size of firm, and job tenure are the main variables which determine wage figures. Besides the difference between men and women, the following three variables are influential on the determination of wages, and thus wage differentials: education, size of firm, and job tenure. The last variable may be replaced by age; alternatively, a combination of job tenure and age can be one main determinant of wages, although the latter is less significant than the former.

These three variables are crucial for the determination of wages only when male data are examined. Male wage figures can provide discrimination-free wage figures. Also, nearly all male observations are unaffected by significant interruptions of labour market activity, unlike female observations. Consequently, the examination of male wage figures can give us a reliable source from which to derive a pure quantitative effect of each variable on wage differentials.

The second conclusion merely indicates that the three variables (or four, if age is included separately) are important for the determination of wages. The economic significance and implications of each variable are described below. Finally, it is noted that a theoretical model of wage determination consisting of only three variables, education, size of firm, and job tenure, is fairly successful in explaining empirical wage figures for male employees who have stayed with the same employers.

(3) Both job tenure and age have particular implications for wage determinations. It is common to believe that the importance of job tenure arises from economic rationality, while that of age arises from a paternalism peculiar to Japan. The former includes the theory of human capital (in particular, specific human capital) and the effort-incentive theory. These two theories are able to show that wages grow with job tenure. Our judgement is that the effort-incentive theory is somewhat more plausible than the specific human-capital theory, in view of the following two observations. First, the slope of wage growth by job tenure is considerably steeper in Japan than in other countries where the specific human-capital argument is applied. The difference in the growth rate of wages between Japan and the rest of world can be attributed to the contribution of the effort-incentive theory. Second, the level of retirement allowances is quite high in Japan. Retirement allowances can be explained by a typical example of the effort-incentive theory.

Our interesting interpretation of the importance of age is the 'living-cost hypothesis', implying that employers pay higher wages to older employees because the latter have greater financial responsibilities. Age is a symbol of the degree of consumption; it is quite natural that the older the age, the higher will be the necessity of expenditure. This hypothesis was tested by Ohta and Tachibanaki (1998), and supported to a certain extent. From a different angle, age may be evaluated on the basis of paternalism. It was found that the influence of job tenure was somewhat stronger than that of age in wage differentials. Therefore, economic rationality (either human capital or effort-incentive) dominates paternalism.

(4) Size of firm has a peculiar effect as a determinant of wages, and the ability-to-pay and/or rent-sharing hypotheses are responsible for the inter-size wage differentials. The reasons for this peculiarity are as follows. First, it was believed that the effect of firm size was the most salient feature of wage differentials, and that it was unique to Japan; there have been controversies concerning the causes and implications of inter-size wage differentials. Second, the influence of firm size on wage differentials is negatively correlated with the movement of business cycles. When the economy is in a boom (or a recession), the wage differential due to size is smaller (or larger). In sum, the differentials are affected by business cycles.

Tachibanaki (1996a) attempted to estimate a pure effect of firm size on wage differentials after controlling for a large number of qualification variables. It obtained the result that a substantial difference remained even after the control; and it was concluded that the ability-to-pay and/or rent-sharing hypotheses were likely to be responsible for this.

One important point regarding the size of firm is that its effect is intrinsic in the determination of wages for the following reason: when the size of firm is used as a control variable, it does substantially reduce the degree of spurious wage differentials by other variables. For example, inter-industry wage differentials were reduced substantially in the presence of firm size as a control variable. And wage differentials between competitive industries and non-competitive (concentrated) industries are explained largely by the wage differentials by the size of firm. In other words, the former industries consist mainly of smaller firms whose wage levels are intrinsically lower, while the latter consist mainly of larger firms whose wage levels are intrinsically higher.

(5) Industrial differences are relatively minor in the determination of wage differentials. Also, the compensating difference in wages is not observed. It is proposed that wage differentials by industries were substantially reduced after controlling for a large number of quality variables. It is possible to conclude, therefore, that the effect of industrial differences

on nominal wage figures, which is very large statistically, is spurious. In other words, pure industrial wage differentials are substantially smaller than spurious industrial wage differentials. See, for example, Tachibanaki (1992a) about the financial industry. The pure inter-size differential is responsible for the spurious inter-industry difference, i.e. between competitive and concentrated sectors.

It is found that the compensating difference in wage payments between industries which have better working conditions and those whose working conditions are worse was not observed. Employees with less favourable working conditions have to accept an additional unfavourable treatment; lower wages. This observation is similar to the case of women, who have to accept several simultaneous and unfavourable treatments in the fields of wages, employments, promotions, etc.

(6) Education (i.e. formal schooling) is an important determinant of wages only for a particular demographic group, notably male white-collar employees. Also, it works as a screening variable for promotion in the firms. Education in Japan has various facets. A notorious social phenomenon is to be found in severe competition for entrance examinations at various stages of formal schooling, from college level even down to elementary school level. It is possible to assume that Japanese people desire to obtain more educational attainment, because this raises earnings capacity considerably. More education here implies two dimensions. The first dimension is to obtain a higher graduation level among various graduation levels such as high schools, junior colleges, universities, and graduate schools, and the second dimension is to enter into a more prestigious school, and, in particular, university.

It is true that Japanese people are anxious to satisfy the above two dimensions. It is important, however, that earnings capacity is not raised by education as much as people in Japan expect: for example, education is significant only for male white-collar workers in the determination of wages; the degree of male/female wage differential would not be narrowed even if the educational level of women were raised. Position in wage distribution is more important than educational attainment in difference in lifetime earnings. See, for example, Tachibanaki (1996a) about the above empirical findings. They suggest that education is not as important for the determination of wages and earnings as people believe or expect. This does not necessarily imply, however, that education does not matter at all; it is true that the average wage is higher when the formal schooling level is higher.

In this sense, education matters to a slight extent in the determination of wages.

How can we assess the role of education in Japan, where the demand for education is incredibly high, under the observed condition that formal education is not so important in raising earnings capacity? One immediate answer is that Japanese people do not know the real story yet, or that they still believe the false hypothesis that education raises earnings capacity considerably.

Several more plausible and scientific answers can be suggested. First, education plays an important role when both occupation and position (hierarchy) in a firm are taken into account. Much more importantly, education determines the occupational attainment to a great extent. See, for example, Tachibanaki (1987b, 1988) in detail.

Second, education performs a screening role in the promotion hierarchy of a firm. Concretely speaking, it was found that only junior college and university graduates could start on the promotion ladder; junior and senior high-school graduates were largely excluded from that entry point. If the top executive level (i.e. board members) is examined, the university from which a candidate for an executive position graduated is significant (see e.g. Tachibanaki, 1998). These two phenomena strongly support the hypothesis that education, both graduation level and name of university, is used as a screening or a filtering device.

Third, education is not yet an extremely important determinant of wages and earnings, contrary to common belief, despite the first and second answers above. Tachibanaki (1996a) provided several reasons why the third point could be proposed. In conclusion, education is a less important determinant of wages and earnings than has popularly been believed, although it does have some effect.

Fourth, it is necessary to add the fact that education is also judged by non-pecuniary standards in Japan; it would require sociological, psychological, and even religious discussions to support this proposition. Several familiar examples are as follows. More education offers a higher chance of making a good marriage. In a family whose members have all completed college education, it may be considered shaming for a member not to possess a college degree. A similar thing may apply in a district where many inhabitants have higher educational qualifications. It is also important to note that some people desire more knowledge and academic achievement without showing any interest in earnings capacity.

(7) Positions (or hierarchies) play a significant role in firms or organizations. In particular, earnings are differentiated by positions to a larger extent.

Internal competition for higher positions is very severe because the number of these positions is limited. Obviously, competition for executive positions is the most severe. See, for example, Tachibanaki (1987b, 1998). One reason for such severe competition arises from the fact that the internal labour market is one of the most salient features in Japan. The effect of the internal labour markets in Japan was evaluated based on international perspectives by Ohashi and Tachibanaki (1998).

Promotion is given mainly to those currently employed in the firm, in particular in larger firms. Severe competition among the same class of entrants to a firm persists for a long period, ten to fifteen years, and possibly longer. Careful monitoring and evaluation of employees are carried out during such a period to select productive employees who can be promoted. Since all junior-college and university graduates among white-collar workers are in line for promotion, all these employees worked hard in expectation of future promotion. We believe that this is one of the reasons for efficient and productive management in large Japanese firms. Blue-collar employees also worked for the same reason, although their final level of promotion will be much lower. It is natural that employers should pay considerably higher wages to employees, both white-collar and blue-collar, who perform well, and who are then promoted.

The above mechanism worked fairly well during the period of strong industrialization and rapid economic growth after the Second World War, when per capita income level was lower. Less-educated employees, who had a smaller chance of promotion because of the screening role of education, also worked hard to receive the highest wages possible, in view of their lower living standard. The Japanese economy produced a high standard of living. Some employees, both educated and less-educated, white-collar and blue-collar, have started to feel dissatisfaction with severe internal competition among employees and with the hard-work ethic (see e.g. Ishikawa, 1994; Tachibanaki, 1996b). The main reason is that Japanese people now enjoy a high level of consumption, except for poor housing in urban areas, and so demand more free time in place of hard working. Thus, it is possible to predict that the growth rate of productivity will decline; some economists, including ourselves, find that signs of this were already apparent a decade ago.

(8) Equality was regarded highly as an acceptable principle in Japanese society. This virtue was operative in many fields of industrial relations and management. Equality (or fairness) has various facets. It happens that a system which is regarded as equality in one country (or society) may be

judged as inequality in another country (or society). Let us take the example of the *nenko joretsu*, or seniority system. This system is judged as equality in Japan because wages grow with employees' length of service. It is fair because everybody can accumulate his or her length of service in one company, regardless of qualifications such as education and occupation and, more importantly, regardless of productivity. This system, however, may be assessed as unfair in the rest of the world because it treats productive and less productive workers equally. This may in fact be unfair; some people believe that productive workers should receive higher wages than less productive workers, even if their length of service is the same.

This equal treatment offers a higher incentive to all employees in Japan; it avoids a disincentive for employees who are treated less favourably, but it may damage the incentive for qualified and productive employees. Japanese society and firms believe that the loss due to the latter outweighs the gain due to the former; consequently, equal treatment of employees has been adopted to seek a higher gain.

We have to add several reservations. First, equality is stressed only among certain group members: males, educated, full-time workers, or workers in larger firms, or other privileged groups. Females, less-educated, part-time workers, or workers in smaller firms, or others, are treated much less favourably. In sum, only the insiders can enjoy the merit of equality. Alternatively speaking, 'equality' benefits the insiders at the expense of the outsiders.

Second, a certain portion of Japanese people have started to think that the Japanese way of equality – such as equal treatment of productive and less productive workers which derives from, for example, the seniority system – is in fact unfair, proposing that it is fair only when the able are rewarded highly and the less able not so highly. Equality may be judged differently as time goes on. This second reservation is crucial in predicting the future course of industrial relations in Japan (see e.g. Tachibanaki, 1992b; 1996b).

5.3 Wage differentials between unionized firms and non-unionized firms

Lewis (1986) concluded that the mean union wage-gap estimates for the US were between 12 and 20 per cent. Booth (1995) concluded that average estimates of the mean union wage-gap from cross-section models were around 15 per cent for the US, and 8 per cent for Britain. They proposed their conclusion based on a large number of empirical estimates.

It is useful to mention the study by Blanchflower and Freeman (1992) who said that the US would be only one country among advanced countries, where the effect of trade unions on various economic variables including wages was positive. What is the situation in Japan?

We estimate the following wage function to draw a pure effect of unions for the data prepared by Rengo-Soken (The Research Institute for Advancement in Living Standards: RIALS), which includes a union dummy variable as an important independent variable. This model takes into account neither a simultaneity problem nor a sample selection problem. This attempt, nevertheless, is useful for the purpose of international comparison because most studies adopted such simple wage functions:

$$\ln W = a_0 + a_1 U + a_2 FS + a_3 T + a_4 S + a_5 DI + a_6 DR1 + a_7 DR2 + a_8 DR3 + a_9 HOUR + u \quad (5.1)$$

where W is monthly wage payment, U is a union dummy variable ($U=1$ if a firm is unionized), FS is size of firm, T is job tenure, S is sales per employee, DI is an industry dummy variable ($DI=1$ if a firm is manufacturing), DRI ($I=1, 2, 3$) is a region dummy, and $HOUR$ is average working hours. Incidentally, W is measured by monthly wage payment as well as per-hour wage payment which is adjusted by regular working hours in the empirical section, and FS is measured by the natural log of the number of employees in a firm. Monthly wage payment includes basic wages, and excludes fringe benefits like family assistance, housing allowance, commuting fee, overtime hours payments, etc.

It is necessary to explain briefly the reasons why these independent variables are used. A brief introduction to wage literature in Japan in the last part explains most of them. Therefore, only a very brief description is provided for each variable.

The job tenure variable is included to take account of the idea of human capital theory. Sales per employee indicates the ability to pay and/or rent-sharing hypotheses. Size of firm in terms of the number of employees in a firm shows the peculiar interest in Japan. Moreover, as shown in Chapter 2, a high correlation between union participation rate and size of firm is observed. Thus, it is desirable to control for the effect of size of firm in order to draw a pure effect of trade unions on wages. A dummy variable for industry and a dummy variable for region need no explanation why they should be included.

We said that gender (male–female difference) and age were important for the determination of wages. We estimate wage functions for data which are separated by both sex and age in order to deal with these characteristics. We pick up observations of both 30-year-old and 45-year-old employees for male and female separately. This implies that the effect of both sex and age is eliminated, and thus it enables us to estimate a pure effect of unions. Finally, it is noted that the job tenure variable is eliminated in the actual estimation because the consideration of employees aged 30 and 45 implies that nearly all employees have common job tenures in view of the fact that we use model wage figures which assume no labour turnovers. Related to this it is necessary to understand that we do not use real wage figures which are paid to existing employees but instead use hypothetical model wages. It is difficult to judge which data sources between real wages and hypothetical wages are more desirable for the purpose of investigating wages.

Several words are added about the treatment of working hours. We include working hours as the independent variable in our model specification. This assumes that the amount of working hours increases the total monthly wage payment which is the dependent variable in this investigation. It is, of course, possible to divide the monthly wage payment by working hours, and regard its hourly wage as the dependent variable. Even in this case it is possible to include working hours as an independent variable, and to attempt to examine whether the compensating balance theory works. This theory, probably, supports the following: 'The longer the working hours, the higher the per-hour wage payment.' Tachibanaki and Ohta (1994) examined these two cases, and found that the compensating balance theory was not supported empirically in Japan. We attempt to examine these two cases for our data source as well.

We use the data source called *Expectation and Effect of Trade Unions*, which was conducted in 1991 by the RIALS (Research Institute of Advancement in Living Standards) with our collaboration. The firms data involved 689 firms, and the response rate was about 10 per cent. Unless some monetary rewards are provided, the response rate in Japan is quite low except for government surveys. Therefore, it is essential to increase the number of questionnaires to have a sufficient number of responses. Nevertheless, we have to keep in mind some degree of selectivity biases. The total number of firms to which the questionnaires were sent was 6,800. Firms were selected randomly. We obtained a sufficient number of replies to enable us to perform econometric studies. There were 308 firms which have unions, and 377 which do not. The union rate is 44.7 per cent, while the non-union rate is 55.3 per cent. Since there are so many smaller firms which are not unionized in Japan, the figure of less than 50 per cent of unionized firms is not surprising at all. The very low rate of union participation in Japan is largely attributable to this low rate of unionized firms among smaller firms.

It is impossible to gather information on unionized firms and non-unionized firms on a national basis. It is, however, possible to obtain information on the rate of union participation (in Japan it is frequently called the union density rate) by employees. *The Fundamental Survey on Labour Unions*, published by the Ministry of Labour, provides the estimated participation rates. The rate is 21.3 per cent for all firms in 1992. The rate of union participation, however, differs greatly according to the size of firms. Larger firms (over 1,000 employees) show a participating rate of 57.2 per cent, middle-size firms (100–999 employees) show 22.5 per cent, and smaller firms show only 1.8 per cent, as was described previously.

The survey used in this work has a higher proportion of smaller firms (i.e., fewer than 299 employees), as will be described later. There is a high positive correlation between the rate of union participation and the rate of union-firms. The figure for the rate of non-union firms, namely 55.3 per cent, may be a somewhat over-representative figure in comparison with the national average of smaller firms. However, it is not an extreme over-representation. Thus, 44.7 per cent versus 55.3 per cent are nearly ideal and balanced figures which enable us to draw pure union effects.

Table 5.1 shows the empirical result of the wage functions estimated by the OLS method. They are estimated for senior high school graduates and university graduates separately as well as the distinction based on sex and age. The result for university graduates and for 45-year-old employees is not presented for the following reasons. First, the result for university graduates is very similar to the result for senior high school graduates. Second, there are a large number of employees among 45-year-old university graduates who were promoted to managerial positions, and thus are not union members currently. It is quite likely that a sample selection bias would be serious for the estimation of the effect of trade unions on wages, if those employees were eliminated. In other words, it would be appropriate to consider only union members even in unionized firms.

Table 5.1 gives the following observations. First, the union dummy variable is not statistically significant for male employees. Even the negative value, which indicates that wages in unionized firms were lower than those in non-unionized firms, was obtained. Since the estimated coefficient, however, is not statistically significant, we do not pay serious attention to it. For female employees, the estimated coefficient

Table 5.1 Estimated results of wage functions for 30-year-old employees

Dependent/ Independent variable	Male senior high			Female senior high		
	Per-hour wages	*Per-hour wages*	*Monthly wages*	*Per-hour wages*	*Per-hour wages*	*Monthly wages*
Constant	1.034**	−0.092*	5.199	1.103**	−0.309**	5.269
	(6.756)	(1.707)	(34.07)	(7.536)	(5.601)	(36.134)
Union dummy U	−0.012	0.008	−0.012	0.006	0.030	−0.005
	(0.698)	(0.467)	(0.713)	(0.313)	(1.489)	(0.287)
Firm size FS	0.020*	0.039**	0.020*	0.026**	0.043**	0.026**
	(2.039)	(3.833)	(2.025)	(2.764)	(4.073)	(2.781)
Sales per employee	0.008	0.023**	0.008	0.017*	0.042**	0.016*
	(0.887)	(2.504)	(0.861)	(1.846)	(4.320)	(1.796)
Industry dummy	−0.053**	−0.052**	−0.052**	−0.067**	−0.064**	−0.065**
	(3.161)	(2.905)	(3.100)	(3.875)	(3.298)	(3.805)
Regional dummy I	0.121**	0.170**	0.120**	0.150**	0.212**	0.148**
	(5.594)	(7.738)	(5.556)	(6.844)	(8.949)	(6.796)
Regional dummy II	0.078**	0.110**	0.077**	0.103**	0.152**	0.102**
	(3.305)	(4.475)	(3.273)	(4.14)	(5.555)	(4.112)
Regional dummy III	0.087**	0.095**	0.087**	0.041	0.047*	0.041
	(3.562)	(3.639)	(3.554)	(1.650)	(1.670)	(1.625)
Regular working hours	−0.0004**		−0.000	−0.001**		
	(7.792)		(0.064)	(10.25)		
Overtime hours	0.000		0.000			
	(0.146)		(0.169)			
R^2	0.273	0.191	0.111	0.444	0.298	0.229

Notes: (1) Figures in parentheses are estimated *t*-values.
(2) *Statistically significant at the 0.1 level, and ** at the 0.05 level.
(3) The OLS (ordinary least squares) method was applied.

is positive with statistical significance. This is consistent with our general understanding, and unions give a benefit to females.

Second, the variables like size of firm, industrial dummy, regional dummy, and sometimes sales per employee are statistically significant. In particular, it is emphasized that size of firm is overwhelmingly significant, and thus it implies the absolute necessity of controlling for the effect of size of firm when we investigate the effect of trade unions on working conditions including wages. The other variables also are statistically significant. The empirical results here reflect the implications of the theory described above, and support our preliminary introduction to wage literatures in Japan. Consequently, no serious economic interpretation is described for each independent variable in Table 5.1.

Table 5.2 Wage differentials between unionized firms and non-unionized firms (%)

	Male				*Female*			
	Senior high		*University*		*Senior high*		*University*	
Age	30	45	30	45	30	45	30	45
Per-hour wages	−1.88	−4.30*	−2.85**	−5.35*	0.56	7.03**	n.a.	n.a.
Monthly wages	−1.21	n.a.	−1.98	n.a.	0.51	4.43	n.a.	n.a.

Notes: (1) * implies statistical significance at the 0.1 level, and ** at the 0.05 level.
(2) The result in this table was calculated based on not only the coefficients in Table 5.1 but also the coefficients for other specifications.
(3) n.a. implies not-available.

Finally, we evaluate the quantitative effect of union/non-union wage differentials. Table 5.2 shows such figures. The plus sign implies that wages in unionized firms are higher than those in non-unionized firms. Female results show the positive signs, while male results show the negative signs. The amount of wage differential in terms of per-hour wage payments is about 1.0–2.5 per cent for 30-year-old employees, and about 4.0–6.0 per cent for 45-year-old employees. It is only about 2.0 per cent in terms of monthly wage payments for the latter.

Table 5.2 shows that observations for employees aged 45 provide statistically significant difference, and that only male university graduates provide statistically significant results among employees aged 30. It shows, however, that wages in unionized firms are lower than those in non-unionized firms. This happened even after several variables which would affect wages were controlled for. This is a somewhat surprising finding in view of the fact that the effect of trade unions on wages is positive, or nil in many countries.

We interpret this unusual result in the following way. Since statistical significance of the union dummy variable is largely unsupported, it is preferable to conclude at this stage that there is no difference in wage payments between unionized firms and non-unionized firms at least for men. This is true even after controls. The female case, however, is different because the effect of unions on wages is likely to be positive. We have to await further empirical results, which take into consideration the problems of simultaneity and/or sample selection, in order to confirm whether or not the above preliminary conclusion is correct.

6
The Effect of Unions and Employee Voice on Wages and Working Conditions: Their Endogeneity Problem

6.1 Introduction

The previous chapter investigated the effect of trade unions on wages as a preliminary analysis by applying a simple equation model. We provided a tentative conclusion that there was no significant union/non-union wage differential for men, while there was a small positive effect of unions on wage premiums for women. This tentative conclusion was obtained under the assumption that there was neither a simultaneous equation problem nor a sample selection problem. It will be useful to examine whether or not such problems would be serious statistically. This chapter attempts to test these problems because possible biases caused by them may change the previous chapter's preliminary conclusion.

The previous chapter examined the effect of unions on wages directly. In other words, wage functions were estimated by introducing a dummy variable of union status. This chapter extends its simple model by considering an intermediary variable, namely the voice of unions, which connects and transmits the effect of trade unions on wages. Another extension in this chapter is to examine the effect of trade unions on not only wages but also various working conditions. The data are briefly explained. We use the RIALS data as the previous chapters used. Table 6.1 shows the summary statistics used in this chapter.

The gender difference suggests that about 80 per cent are male, while 20 per cent are female. The share of male employees is about 10 percentage points higher in union firms than that in non-union firms. The average age of all male employees is 37.6-years-old, and the average job tenure is 11.7 years. They are 38.9-years-old and 13.9 years respectively for union firms, while they are 36.5-years-old and 9.7 years respectively for non-union firms. It is found that both age and job

Table 6.1 Means and standard deviations of the variables adopted in our sample

		Union	*Non-union*
Male tenure (years)		13.9	9.7
		(4.84)	(4.63)
Male age (years)		38.9	36.5
		(4.95)	(5.20)
Ratio of female to male employment (%)		0.223	0.437
		(0.70)	(0.95)
Employment number		904	197
		(1784)	(277)
Monthly wage (000 yen)	U	230.1	233.3
		(43.43)	(39.78)
	S	215.7	215.7
		(38.84)	(35.48)
Monthly wage adjusted regular working hours (000 yen)	U	1.382	1.353
		(0.280)	(0.250)
	S	1.298	1.252
		(0.268)	(0.233)
Regular working hours		2007.2	2079.8
		(144.9)	(152.6)
Overtime working hours		231.5	237.7
		(164.1)	(172.2)
Paid holidays		16.19	14.14
		(3.013)	(2.646)
Ratio of paid holidays		0.577	0.588
		(0.290)	(0.210)
Severance payment (0000 yen)	U	14804	13116
		(539.9)	(582.4)
	S	13007	11452
		(501.7)	(504.2)
Per capita sales (ten million yen)		6.07	5.57
		(9.337)	(8.904)

Notes: U signifies university graduates, and S signifies senior high school graduates. Wages are measured for thirty-year-old employees who have never changed employers after graduating from schools.

tenure in union-firms are older and longer than non-union firms by 2.4 years and 4.2 years respectively, reflecting the fact that lower turnover rates are observed in union-firms.

6.2 Endogeneity problem and union effects

6.2.1 Endogeneity

If the problem of union status endogeneity were serious, the ordinarily least squares estimate, which was used in Chapter 5, would be biased.

In other words, the correlation between the union dummy variable and the error term would cause a bias. Two alternative approaches to overcome such a problem are instrumental variables (IV) and control function methods. Duncan and Leigh (1985) suggested some special assumptions which warrant consistency of the estimate by IV. We apply a Wu-Hausman test which examines the null hypothesis of exogeneity of union status. Control function methods were applied by Robinson and Tomes (1984), and Robinson (1989). We would like to apply this method to examine whether or not sample selectivity in either union firms or non-union firms is evident.

Before presenting the estimated results, the theoretical model is presented and discussed briefly. The model consists of the following three equations:

$$q_i = X_i \pi + \epsilon_i \quad (6.1)$$
$$\ln W_{ui} = X_{ui} \alpha_u + \epsilon_{ui} \quad (6.2)$$
$$\ln W_{ni} = X_{ni} \alpha_n + \epsilon_{ni} \quad (6.3)$$

Equations (6.2) and (6.3) are wage functions for the union firms and non-union firms, respectively. Thus, subscript u stands for unions, and n stands for non-unions. The vector X_i (the explanatory variables) is the same as the explanatory variables in equation (5.1) in Chapter 5 which eliminates the union dummy variable U. Equation (6.1) is a reduced-form threshold (selection) equation obtained by substituting the wage functions into a structural union status equation. q_i is an unobserved latent variable, and its dichotomous realization U_i is the observed union status. If $q_i > 0$, U_i is set equal to one, indicating that the i-th firm is unionized and the observed wage W_i is W_{ui}. If $q_i \leqq 0$, U_i is set equal to zero, indicating that the i-th firm is non-unionized and the observed wage W_i is W_{ni}.

The wage figure W_i is written as follows:

$$\ln W_i = \alpha_n + (\alpha_u - \alpha_n)\, U_i + X\beta + V_i \quad (6.4)$$
$$V_i = \epsilon_{ni} + (\epsilon_{ui} - \epsilon_{ni}) U_i \quad (6.5)$$

Given joint normality of ε_i, ε_{ui} and ε_{ni} and assuming $\text{var}(\varepsilon_i) = 1$, (6.1), (6.2) and (6.3) yield the following modification to (6.4):

$$\begin{aligned} \ln W_i = {} & \alpha_n + (\alpha_u - \alpha_n)\, U_i + X\beta + \sigma\,(\epsilon_{ni}, \epsilon_i)\, \lambda_{ni} \\ & + [\sigma(\epsilon_{ui}, \epsilon_i) - \sigma(\epsilon_{ni}, \epsilon_i)]\, \lambda_{ui}\, U_i + V_i \end{aligned} \quad (6.6)$$

where

$$\lambda_i = \begin{cases} \lambda_{ui} & \text{if } U_i = 1 \\ \lambda_{ni} & \text{if } U_i = 0 \end{cases}$$

and λ_{ui} and λ_{ni} are the relevant inverse Mills ratios. The selectivity bias term involves ratios and $-f(X_i\hat{\pi})/F(X_i\hat{\pi})$ and $f(X_i\hat{\pi})/[1-F(X_i\hat{\pi})]$ where, $f(\cdot)$ and $F(\cdot)$ are, respectively, the density and distribution function of a standard normal variable, and the estimates are probit estimates obtained in the first stage. The empirical analysis is attempted by adopting this two-step procedure, and examines whether or not the selectivity variable is statistically significant. If the selectivity variable turned out to be insignificant, the endogeneity problem would not matter.

Another method which is capable of examining the union endogeneity problem is to apply a Wu-Hausman exogeneity test. Duncan and Leigh (1985) suggested a test procedure, namely equation (6.7):

$$\ln W_i = Z_i\beta + \hat{Z}_i\,\gamma + \phi_i \tag{6.7}$$

where $Z_i = (Z_{ui}, Z_{ni}) = (U_i\, X_{ui}, (1-U_i)\, X_{ni})$, $\beta_i = (\beta_u, \beta_n)$, and $\hat{Z}_i$ is a vector of instruments defined as $\hat{Z}_i = [(X_{ui}\hat{U}_i), (X_{ni}\,(1-\hat{U}_i)]$. The test is performed for the hypothesis of $\gamma = 0$ in (6.7).

Table 6.2 shows the result of the wage functions which were estimated by the two-step procedure. The estimated standard errors are adjusted. Thus, they can show appropriate figures for testing. The wage figures are regular monthly wage payments which are adjusted by working hours. We used monthly wage payments without adjusting for working hours as an alternative measure for the wage variable. We obtained similar conclusions based on the two different measurements for wages, although it was natural that the independent variable, namely working hours, was not statistically significant in the case in which regular monthly wage was used as the dependent variable. Two samples, namely (1) senior high school graduates and (2) university graduates, are male 30-year-olds, and they are estimated separately.

The most important finding derived from this table is the statistical insignificance of two selectivity bias terms (i.e., both union firms and non-union firms). The table suggests that both of the estimated coefficients on Select are small in relation to their estimated standard errors. In other words, the ratios of the estimated coefficients over their standard errors are small. It is important to note that the null hypothesis of exogeneity is equivalent to the hypothesis that the inverse Mills ratio terms (i.e., Select variables) do not enter into the regression. This insignificance leads to the conclusion that selection bias is not observed in wage functions. The wage distribution in union firms or non-union firms is not significantly different from the wage distribution that would be observed for a firm selected randomly from the

Table 6.2 Estimated wage function

Independent variable	*Male senior high school graduates whose ages are 30-years-old*		*Male college graduates whose ages are 30-years-old*	
	(1)(a)	*(2)(b)*	*(3)(a)*	*(4)(b)*
Constant	0.997**	5.162**	1.121**	5.281**
	(5.563)	(30.51)	(6.022)	(29.67)
Union	−0.005	−0.003	−0.026	−0.025
	(0.947)	(0.066)	(0.889)	(0.813)
Firm Size	0.020**	0.020**	0.022**	0.021**
	(2.171)	(2.157)	(2.121)	(2.105)
Sales per Employee	0.009	0.008	−0.027**	−0.028**
	(1.016)	(0.983)	(2.743)	(2.717)
Industry Dummy	−0.050**	−0.048**	−0.014	−0.013
	(3.127)	(3.061)	(0.853)	(0.820)
Regional Dummy I	0.117**	0.116**	0.111**	0.110**
	(5.711)	(5.694)	(5.377)	(5.312)
II	0.081**	0.080**	0.052**	0.052**
	(3.591)	(3.566)	(2.103)	(2.080)
III	0.086**	0.086**	0.047*	0.047*
	(3.584)	(3.594)	(1.884)	(1.890)
Hours (regular) (c)	−0.050**	0.006	−0.050**	−0.012
	(6.728)	(0.076)	(6.012)	(0.142)
Hours (overtime) (c)	−0.010	0.012	−0.010	0.050
	(0.214)	(0.196)	(0.728)	(0.711)
Select I (Non-union) (d)	−0.026	−0.028	−0.017	−0.018
	(0.724)	(0.761)	(0.672)	(0.684)
Select II (Union) (d)	0.032	0.032	0.054	0.053
	(0.883)	(0.892)	(1.456)	(1.462)
AdjR^2	0.279	0.091	0.244	0.082

Notes: (1) (a) Dependent variables in columns (1) and (3) are monthly wage payments which are adjusted by working hours.
(2) (b) Dependent variables in columns (2) and (4) are monthly wage payments without adjusting for working hours.
(3) Figures in parentheses are the asymptotic t-ratios.
(4) * implies statistical significance at the 0.1 level, and ** at the 0.05 level.
(5) (c) Coefficient are multiplied by 100.
(6) (d) Select I and Select II are the inverse Mills ratio. They imply selectivity bias terms.

subsample of union firms and non-union firms which have the common firm characteristics.

6.2.2 Other findings on the effect on wages

Other observations in Table 6.2 are as follows. First, the union coefficients give the negative coefficients. Since these negative values were statistically insignificant, we understand that there is no significant difference between union firms and non-union firms regarding wage payments.

Second, it is necessary to explain the reason why the effect of working hours on per-hour wage payment is negative. We understand that this is caused by decreasing working hours in the early 1990s in Japan. The reduction in working hours was the national goal in view of very long working hours compared with other countries, and thus employers were unable to cut per-hour wage figures for fear of employees' resistance, or to keep their work incentive. This implies that the per-hour wages are increased under the constant monthly wages, when working hours are decreased. This is the main reason for the negative coefficient.

Third, one surprising result appears in the negative coefficient of sales per employee for 30-year-old university graduates. It is possible to raise one conjecture: wages are determined for university graduates regardless of the firm's sales, i.e., revenue value, because the firm determines their wages based on the long-run personnel management policy for these graduates.

It should be useful to cite the study by Brunello (1992) who obtained the negative effect of unions on wages in Japan. Brunello's study did not control for the contribution of firm size, education and job tenure to the wage determination nor take account of working hours, although the main virtue of his study is the examination of the micro data on the effect of unions on productivity, profit rate and wages. Since wages are affected by many elements, the control attempted by us is able to show a convincing result. Nevertheless, it is worthwhile to repeat that the two studies produced a similar conclusion in the sense that a positive effect of unions on wages was not obtained. Tsuru and Rebitzer (1995) and Noda (1997b) also obtained a similar result, although the data source is totally different.

It may be useful to summarize the reason for obtaining no strong evidence on union wage differentials in Japan. First, even if the effect of unions was positive for raising employees' wages, non-union firms would follow the wage outcome of union firms. In other words, non-union firms also will increase the wages of their employees almost immediately because they are afraid of employee dissatisfaction. This is called the spillover effect. The most useful theory is, probably, the efficiency wage hypothesis, or the 'fair' wage hypothesis because it can explain why non-union firms increase wages. Workers are cautious in a possible discrepancy between the prevailing market wage and their own wages. If such a discrepancy were found to be large due to an increase in wages in union firms, the disincentive effect in non-union firms would be significant.

Second, the famous *Shunto* (spring offensive) in Japan, which negotiates wage determination annually, argues the increase (or decrease) in the average wage payment of all employees based mainly on the past macro performance such as productivity, inflation rate and other factors. Thus, the wage determination based on individual firms' and/or individual employees' performance has been only a secondary concern. Also, employers have tried to minimize the distribution of wages among employees to keep work incentives for all employees. See, for example, Sano (1969) and Tachibanaki (1996a). Therefore, the Shunto does not necessarily consider the difference between union firms and non-union firms.

Third, labour conditions, such as recruitment, dismissals, internal transfer, promotion, changes in production technique and fundamental management policy, working hours, daily working conditions at offices or factories, which are the important subjects demanded by union members, are discussed at the negotiations. See Tachibanaki and Noda (1996) about the effect of unions on these matters. This implies that wages are not always the first priority of trade unions.

A word is added here about the effect of job tenure, age, education and gender on wages. Since we have controlled for the effect of these variables, it is not easy to draw the difference in the influence of these variables between union firms and non-union firms. We do not deny, however, that the above subject is important. Finally, it is noted that a similar result was obtained regarding the effect of unions on wages, even if annual wage earnings including bonus were used.

6.2.3 Statistical test

Going back to the issue of endogeneity, it is concluded, based on the above analyses, that it is not necessary to take into account the endogeneity problem of unions and the sample selection problem in Japan when we investigate 'union wage differentials'. It is possible to present supplementary evidence which supports the conclusion based on statistical tests.

The first statistical test is the comparison between instrumental variables in (6.7) and ordinary least squares, and the second test is the comparison between inverse Mills ratios and ordinary least squares. The first is the famous Wu-Hausman test, and the second is the usual joint significance test.

The estimated statistics, namely F-value, is 1.029 for senior high school graduates and 0.210 for college graduates, respectively, in the Wu-Hausman test. These values are much smaller than the critical values at relevant significance levels. The estimated statistics, namely F-value for the joint test of the inverse is 1.190 for senior high school graduates and 0.415 for college graduates, respectively. These figures also are smaller than the relevant critical values, and the result implies no selection bias. Thus, we can safely estimate pure union differential by ordinary least squares.

It is possible to interpret this result in the following way. The decision to form trade unions and/or participate in trade unions is made without seriously considering whether unions affect wages or other working conditions. The decision is influenced by other factors such as strong union movement by several leaders, closed-shops, cheap union fees, and others, as discussed in detail by Tachibanaki (1993).

6.2.4 Effect on other working conditions

It would be interesting to inquire into the effect of unions on non-wage labour market conditions such as working hours, and paid holidays, etc. under the condition of the endogeneous determinations. No study has examined these issues in Japan. First, the effect on regular working hours is examined. It is noted again that the estimated standard errors are adjusted. Table 6.3 shows the estimated result. The dummy variable on unions is negative with statistical significance, implying that working hours in union firms are shorter than in non-union firms. In view of the estimated coefficient the difference in working hours is approximately 5.3 per cent between them. By combining this result with the previous result, i.e., the negative effect of working hours on per-hour wages, it is possible to speculate that Japanese unions raised wages significantly by reducing regular working hours.

Second, a similar result was obtained for severance payments. The union dummy is positive with statistical significance. The difference between union firms and non-union firms with regard to the amount of severance payments is about 28 per cent. The severance payment system encourages workers to stay longer in the firm, and enables them to accumulate more firm-specific human capital. The main reason is that the Japanese severance payment system gives a penalty in the amount of payment if employees stop their careers in one firm. In other words, the longer the job tenure, the larger the amount of severance payment. The result is obtained for both university and senior higher school graduates whose job tenures are 35 years.

Table 6.3 Estimated labour condition function

Independent variable	*Regular working hours*	*Severance payments (a)*
Constant	7.731**	6.119**
	(34.95)	(38.98)
Union	−0.054**	0.252**
	(4.199)	(2.191)
Firm size	−0.012**	0.108**
	(2.992)	(3.533)
Sales per employee	−0.015**	0.163**
	(5.334)	(6.341)
Industry dummy	0.009*	−0.027
	(1.670)	(0.060)
Regional dummy I	−0.055**	0.217**
	(7.700)	(4.114)
II	−0.022**	0.066
	(2.818)	(0.869)
III	−0.011	−0.019
	(1.580)	(0.304)
Select I (Non-union) (b)	0.015	0.050
	(1.145)	(0.435)
Select II (Union) (b)	0.006	−0.123
	(0.387)	(0.923)
AdjR^2	0.291	0.248

Notes: (1) (a) Severance payment for university graduates whose job tenure is 35 years.
(2) (b) Select I and select II are the inverse Mills ratio. They imply selectivity bias terms.
(3) Figures in parentheses are the asymptotic t-ratios.
(4) * implies statistical significance at the 0.10 level, and ** at the 0.05 level.

Third, the effect on both the number of paid holidays and overtime working hours is not statistically significant. Thus, the effect of unions on these variables is negligible. Therefore, the empirical result is not presented here to save space.

In sum, it is possible to conclude that there is a positive effect of unions on several non-wage working conditions, although the effect on wages is negligible. We performed various statistical tests to examine whether or not the endogeneity problem was serious. Although the empirical result is not reported here due to space limitation, it was found that the endogeneity problem was not serious. Finally, it is noted that a similar result was obtained for the sample which excludes firms with more than 1,000 employees. Thus, our result is valid regardless of the size of firm.

6.3 The effect of voices: union firms versus non-union firms

6.3.1 Voices of employees

This section examines the effect of the voices of employees on various labour conditions such as working hours, separations and other conditions. Wages also are examined later. The survey which was used in this study asked several questions on 'How strong are the voices of employees on various management conditions?' 'Voices' may be interpreted as the bargaining power of employees on various management issues. Several economists representatively given by Freeman (1980a), Freeman and Medoff (1984) emphasized the voice of unions in interpreting a lower turnover rate of employees among union members.

In the previous section, we examined the effect of unions on not only wages but also several non-wage working conditions, by employing an endogenous dummy variable. This method is not perfect for investigating the effect of unions. For example, it is possible to find a case in which the existence of unions does not necessarily strengthen the opinion and desire of union members. In an extreme case, a union may demand nothing of its employer, even if it is organized by many members. Simply, a union is dead even if a union takes unity in the previous dummy variable classification. This example suggests the necessity that some degree of union voices, or the power of unions is taken into consideration, when the intrinsic effect of unions ought to be measured.

Although it is quite possible to conceive of the fact that unions would raise the degree of the voices substantially, it is misleading to presume that employees in non-union firms have no voices, or no bargaining powers against their employers. In the other extreme case, employees even in non-union firms can demand many things from employers for various reasons. 'Employee associations' or some other organizations in Japan, which are not equivalent to conventional unions, engage in negotiations with employers. Even without any formal 'employee associations' it is likely that employees will present their demand to employers, and they have some voices, or bargaining powers, although the extent of powers may be less than in union firms. In sum, the degree of the voices or the bargaining powers in non-union firms is not zero, but would differ from that in union firms. The previous union dummy classification assumes that the voice of non-union firms is zero. This is somewhat unrealistic for the reasons described above. In other words, there is a case in which the voice of employees in non-union firms is stronger than that of union firms. Thus, it is desirable to construct the variable which indicates the intrinsic power of employees which is separated from the conventional zero-one union dummy. Therefore, it would be interesting to inquire whether or not the voices work differently between union firms and non-union firms. We will examine the influence of the voices for union firms and non-union firms separately.

6.3.2 Quantification of the voices and estimation method

We adopt the following method to quantify the voice of unions, or the power of unions. When there is no union in the firm, it is the voice of employees rather than the voice of unions. The survey prepared four different levels of answers to the question of whether or not employees express their opinions or desires to employers with respect to the eight management and labour conditions described below. The four different levels are as follows. Employees express them (1) strongly, (2) somewhat strongly, (3) marginally, and (4) there is no room for expressing them – in other words, employers do not listen to employees' demands. The numerical value three was given to (1) strongly, and two, one and zero was given in descending order, respectively.

Our statistical method which considers the intermediary variable, the voice, can take account of the situation where employers do not listen to strong demand by employees. The other extreme case is that employers take into account even weak demand by employees. Of course, there is a case in which employers take account of strong demand by employees. In other words, we should like to judge which case is more plausible among the above different cases. In sum, this variable indicates the degree of employers' cooperativeness towards employees, or willingness to listen to employees' demand, although it is judged by employers subjectively. It might be desirable to measure it objectively to obtain a more reliable result. We believe, nevertheless, that the subjective judgment is valuable.

'What kind of management and labour conditions are requested and disputed among various conditions?' There are a total of eight conditions which were prepared for this survey. They are (1) training, (2) bonus and wage, (3) daily management matters which happen at offices and factories usually, or working conditions at working places, (4) non-wage welfare system such as housing, medical care, etc. (5) holiday and working hours, (6) mandatory retirement, (7) transfer of employees in both section and establishment, and sending employees off to group companies, i.e., *keiretsu* firms which are tied by common capital, or by supplier relations, and (8) management policy, production and sales planning at higher levels.

There is one problem when we examine the effect of the voice of employees based on our method. It is likely that the voice of employees on holiday and working hours will affect directly the determination of these variables. It is, however, possible to conceive of the following indirect effect: even if the direct effect on working hours is small, it is possible to shorten working hours when the employee voice on management policy, production and sales planning contributes to efficient management in the firm. In other words, there are various channels forming multiple voices, which affect one working condition, say working hours. Also, it is possible that each channel cannot be identified. In view of the above difficulty, we adopt the following two methods to measure the voice of employees. The first is to take the average value of the eight conditions, and the second is to take each condition independently and separately. It would be interesting to compare a possible different outcome between the two measurement methods. Anyway, our method enables us to investigate the various degrees of union effect rather than only the zero-one difference in union effect.

Table 6.4 shows the average, and standard deviation of the eight variables, which was quantified above, for union firms and non-union firms. The result suggests that the voice of employees is stronger in union firms than non-union firms. It should be noted, nevertheless,

Table 6.4 Difference in the voices of employees between union firms and non-union firms

	Union firms *Mean (SD)*	*Non-union firms* *Mean (SD)*
Education and training	1.560 (0.905)	1.480 (0.920)
Wage and bonus payment	2.506 (0.748)	1.416 (1.078)
Improvement in daily management matters	2.033 (0.755)	1.927 (0.723)
Fringe benefit	2.164 (0.758)	1.802 (0.862)
Holiday and working hours	2.412 (0.748)	1.716 (0.977)
Mandatory retirement and employment of older workers	1.677 (1.006)	0.941 (0.876)
Worker re-allocation and transfer	1.422 (1.092)	1.272 (0.966)
Management policy, production and sales planning at higher levels	1.449 (1.066)	1.343 (1.012)
Average value of the eight conditions	1.820 (0.485)	1.430 (0.561)

that even non-union firms have some positive degree of the voice because the average is over unity. Employees who do not organize unions can express their opinions through various channels such as 'employee associations'.

When we examine each condition separately, it is found that (2) bonus and wages, (4) non-wage welfare system, (5) holiday and working hours, have higher scores, while (7) transfer and sending, (8) management policy, production and sales planning at higher levels have lower scores. This is quite natural because employees are concerned with their working conditions much more than with management policies at higher levels.

The model is briefly presented here. It is basically an inverse Mills ratio model. Various labour conditions *WC* is explained by a vector of *X*, *VOICE* and selectivity bias terms. A vector of *X* consists of firm size, region, industry, and sales per employee. Specifically, the model is written as follows:

$$I_i = X_i p + e_i \tag{6.8}$$
$$WC_{ui} = X_{ui} q_u + b_u VOICE_{ui} + h_{ui} \tag{6.9}$$
$$WC_{ni} = X_{ni} q_n + b_n VOICE_{ni} + h_{ni} \tag{6.10}$$

where the subscript u signifies union firms, and n signifies non-union firms. p, q_u, q_n, b_u, and b_n are the parameters to be estimated. I_i is an unobserved latent variable, which is used for the first-stage probit estimate. If the selection adjustment is considered, (6.9) and (6.10) may be rewritten as follows:

$$WC_{ui} = X_{ui}\,\theta_u + \beta_u VOICE_{ui} + \sigma_{\epsilon u}\frac{-f(X_i\hat{\pi})}{F(X_i\hat{\pi})} + \delta_{ui} \tag{6.11}$$

$$WC_{ni} = X_{ni}\,\theta_n + \beta_n VOICE_{ni} + \sigma_{\epsilon n}\frac{f(X_i\hat{\pi})}{[1 - F(X_i\hat{\pi})]} + \delta_{ni} \tag{6.12}$$

where $f(\cdot)$ and $F(\cdot)$ are, respectively, the density and distribution functions of a standard normal variable. e_i and h_{ui}, h_{ni}, are distributed joint-normally, and we assume $\text{var}(e_i) = 1$. $\lambda_u = -f(X_i\hat{\pi})/F(X_i\hat{\pi})$ and $\lambda_n = f(X_i\hat{\pi})/[1 - F(X_i\hat{\pi})]$ may be specified.

Five dependent variables are used to estimate the model given by (6.8), (6.9), (6.10), (6.11) and (6.12). These dependent variables which indicate various categories of labour conditions are (1) regular working hours, (2) severance payment, (3) paid holidays, (4) overtime working hours, and (5) the rate of paid holidays, and each dependent variable is used separately. We take the log-form for each variable except for

(3) and (5). Finally, (6) the rate of separations is estimated based on the usual ordinary least squares method and 2SLS. However, several independent variables are added in the case of the rate of separations because it is anticipated that the rate of separations would be influenced by many factors. These additional explanatory variables are (1) average age of employees, (2) wage profile, (3) regular working hours, (4) paid holidays, (5) severance payment and several others. Wage profile here signifies the slope of wage curves with age or job tenure.

6.3.3 Empirical results on non-wage labour conditions

Table 6.5 shows the empirical results. We use the adjusted standard errors. We do not provide detailed interpretations on the effect of independent variables on labour conditions to save space. However, the subjects associated with the difference between union firms and non-union firms, the influence of the voices, and the implication of selection variable are examined in detail. We do not provide below any interpretations on the effect of female ratios, average ages and job tenures because the estimated coefficients are statistically insignificant.

As for regular working hours, the effect of the voices of employees in union firms is negative with statistical significance, while it is negative but statistically insignificant in non-union firms. The stronger the voices of employees in union firms, the shorter are the working hours in these firms. The estimated coefficient indicates that a one-point increase in the voice decreases regular working hours by 1.4 per cent. The above result is not observed in non-union firms. Negative selectivity is seen because the positive coefficient is obtained at the selection variable in union firms. Also, the coefficient is significant statistically. The negative coefficient in non-union firms, however, is not significant. Thus, it is impossible to assert any selectivity with confidence.

A similar result is obtained for severance payment, namely the higher the voices of employees in union firms, the higher the amount of severance payment. A one-point increase in the voice increases severance payments by 15 per cent. Non-union firms, however, do not show any effect because the estimated coefficient of *VOICE* is insignificant statistically. The selection variables are statistically insignificant both in union firms and non-union firms. Therefore, selectivity bias does not matter for severance payment. No different result was obtained between university graduates and senior high graduates regarding this effect.

As for the number of paid holidays, it is found that the voices of employees have a positive effect in both union firms and non-union firms. In other words, there is no difference between union firms and

Table 6.5 The effect of the voices on working conditions

Independent variable	*Regular working hours*		*Severance payment (a)*		*Paid holidays*	
	Union	*Non-union*	*Union*	*Non-union*	*Union*	*Non-union*
Constant	7.672**	7.825**	6.278**	6.066**	23.37**	7.882**
	(237.5)	(205.5)	(22.38)	(18.61)	(0.474)	(5.066)
Firm size	−0.006	−0.027**	0.084**	0.175**	0.379**	0.784**
	(1.621)	(3.861)	(3.135)	(3.362)	(2.514)	(3.041)
Sales per employee	−0.015**	−0.015**	0.142**	0.197**	0.644**	0.634**
	(4.254)	(3.671)	(2.791)	(4.745)	(3.166)	(2.832)
Voice	−0.014**	−0.007	0.144**	0.024	0.623*	0.577**
	(2.091)	(1.131)	(2.729)	(0.408)	(1.715)	(1.680)
λ (b)(c)	0.030**	−0.021	−0.099	0.354	−12.22	−0.667
	(2.968)	(0.006)	(0.449)	(1.581)	(0.233)	(0.610)
AdjR^2	0.263	0.273	0.191	0.202	0.066	0.081

Independent variable	*Over time working hours*		*Rate of paid holidays*	
	Union	*Non-union*	*Union*	*Non-union*
Constant	5.549**	5.029**	1.556	0.973**
	(8.452)	(6.803)	(0.528)	(3.214)
Firm size	0.119*	0.045	−0.021	−0.069**
	(1.882)	(0.368)	(1.383)	(3.060)
Sales per employee	−0.127	−0.001	−0.077	−0.060
	(1.054)	(0.001)	(0.070)	(1.416)
Voice	−0.043	0.050	−0.005	0.033
	(0.358)	(0.368)	(0.582)	(1.257)
λ	−0.695	0.681	−0.468	−0.211
	(1.200)	(1.359)	(0.398)	(0.441)
AdjR^2	0.015	0.002	0.050	0.100

Notes: (1) (a) Severance payment for university graduates whose job tenures are 35 years.
(2) (b)λ signifies the inverse Mills ratio. They imply selectivity bias terms.
(3) (c) Coefficient multiplied by 100.
(4) Figures in parentheses are the asymptotic t-ratios.
(5) *implies statistical significance at the 0.10 level, and ** at the 0.05 level.

non-union firms with respect to the influence of the voices on the determination of paid holidays.

As for overtime working hours and the rate of paid holidays, it was found that the effect of the voices (or the bargaining powers)

Table 6.6 The effect of the voices on wage for university graduates (a)

Independent variable	*Unions firms*	*Non-union firms*
Voices	−0.024	0.003
	(0.904)	(0.164)
λ (b)	−0.005	0.006
	(0.087)	(0.126)
AdjR^2	0.228	0.234

Notes: (1)(a) Dependent variables are monthly wage payments which are adjusted by working hours.
(2)(b) λ signifies the inverse mills ratio. They imply selectivity bias terms.
(3) Figures in parentheses are the asymptotic *t*-ratios.

of employees was not influential on these labour conditions because the estimated coefficients of the voice variables are statistically insignificant.

We will now examine the effect of the voice of employees on wages. To save space we will report only the result for 30-year-old university graduates. Table 6.6 shows the estimated result. Incidentally, the result for 30-year-old senior high school graduates is similar to the result for university graduates. The estimated coefficients for the voice variable are not statistically significant both for union firms and non-union firms. The voice of employees does not affect wages, and there is no relation with whether or not unions are organized. Section 6.2 presented the result such that unions did not affect wages. It is useful to conclude that the examination of the voice variable showed a consistent result with the examination of unions regarding their effect on wages. It confirms no relationship between unions and wages.

An interesting difference, however, appears when the effect of the voice of employees on non-wage labour conditions was examined, because the voice for union firms did matter, while the voice for non-union firms had no effect on regular working hours and severance payments. This suggests that the difference in non-wage labour conditions between union firms and non-union firms is attributed to the fact that the voice of employees affects the working conditions more significantly in union firms than non-union firms.

The overall result based on the model, which considers the intermediary variable, i.e., the voice of employees, is consistent with the result based on the union versus non-union dummy variable. It is important, nevertheless, to point out the fact that the stronger the voice of employees in union firms, the larger the effect on regular working hours and severance payment, while there is no effect on working conditions in non-union firms regardless of the degree of the voice of employees. This implies that the effect of unions is stronger intrinsically than that of non-union firms even if both sides have the same degree of voices.

We prepared five tables in which each separated voice variable on each condition is considered independently as the explanatory variable. These tables are not presented here to save space. (They are available on request to the authors.) Only the result is described here. First, we examine the effect on severance payment. Although the voice on non-wage welfare system has a positive effect on severance payment, the voice on mandatory retirement has a negative effect. Our interpretation for the above is that prolonging mandatory retirement age accompanies a negative effect on per-capita severance payment. The voice on management policies at higher levels has a positive effect because it is likely to raise a firm's overall performance. When we examine non-union firms, the result is similar to the case in union firms regarding the sign of each voice variable. The magnitude of the estimated coefficient, however, is nearly the same if we consider their absolute values. The effect of the average of the eight variables had no influence previously because the positive and negative effects of the eight variables cancelled out. The voice on management policies at higher levels is not statistically significant.

As for the effect on working hours, the voice on holiday, vacation and working hours, and management policies at higher levels, respectively has a positive effect in union firms. It is possible that efficient management caused by the voice on management policies enabled the firm to reduce working hours. Incidentally, no effect is observed in non-union firms.

As for the effect on paid holidays, the voice on holiday and working hours has a positive effect in both union and non-union firms. The effect on overtime working hours and the rate of paid holidays, however, is not observed. These results are consistent with the previous one which used the average of the eight conditions.

It is noted that we examined also two different methods for the voice variable for the wage function. The result shows no effect of the voice on wages in both union and non-union firms. It was found at the same time that there are multiple channels or voices which affect the degree of even one working condition. It would not be feasible to obtain these results, as we considered only the union versus non-union dummy variable.

Table 6.7 The result of t-test on the difference in the rate of separation (%)

Union firms		*Non-union firms*		*t-value*
Mean	*SD*	*Mean*	*SD*	
5.56	5.35	7.83	5.63	3.82

6.3.4 Effect on separations

Finally, the effect on the rate of separations is examined. Here, the rate of separations is measured by the difference between annual separations and annual retirements over total employments for male workers. We will examine only the male observations because female turnovers are affected by many factors. It is noted, nevertheless, that male–female combined observations did not provide us with radically different results. Thus, they are not included here. Table 6.7 shows the mean, standard deviation and t-test of the rate of separations for union firms and non-union firms. It indicates that the rate of separations is lower by 2.3 percentage points for union firms than non-union firms, and the difference is statistically significant. As the US study, for example, given by Freeman and Medoff (1984) shows, unions lower the rate of separation significantly also in Japan.

What happens to labour separations if the effect of the voice of employees is considered? The estimated result is presented in Table 6.8. Since the result based on 2SLS is not different from that based on OLS, we present only the OLS result in Table 6.8. There are several distinctions between union firms and non-union firms with respect to the effect of the explanatory variables.

First, the voices of employees in union firms are negatively influential, while those in non-union firms have no significant effect on separations. The louder the voices in union firms, the lower the rate of separations in labour turnover. The estimated coefficient indicates that a one point increase in the voice decreases the rate of separations by 1.5 percentage point. We conducted the same experiment, i.e., adopting each separated variable independently like the previous one. We obtained no significant effect of each separated variable on separations. Thus, it is concluded that each separated variable does not affect separations.

Second, severance payment has a negative effect in union firms, while it has no significant effect in non-union firms because the estimated coefficient is insignificant statistically. It should be pointed out, however,

Table 6.8 The effect of various labour conditions and voices on the rate of separation (a)

Independent variable	*Union firms*		*Non-union firms*	
Constant	15.52*	24.86**	12.10	15.19**
	(1.747)	(6.354)	(0.089)	(2.448)
Sales per employee	−0.329	−0.433	−0.774	−1.046
	(0.756)	(0.965)	(1.198)	(1.440)
Average age	−0.015*	−0.017**	−0.002	−0.001
	(1.903)	(2.115)	(0.195)	(0.057)
Wage profile (b)	−3.566**		−4.562**	
	(2.298)		(2.385)	
Regular hours	0.006**		0.008*	
	(2.100)		(1.860)	
Paid holidays	−0.391**	−0.356**	−0.405	−0.473*
	(2.853)	(2.518)	(1.841)	(1.918)
Severance payment (c)		−0.002**		−0.002
		(2.278)		(1.424)
Voices	−1.495**	−1.443*	0.680	0.429
	(2.020)	(1.905)	(0.681)	(0.365)
AdjR^2	0.186	0.153	0.114	0.075

Notes: (1) The rate of separation is measured by the difference between annual separations and annual retirements over total number employments for male workers.
(2)(b) Wage Profiles is measured by the ratio of 45-years-old's wages over 30-years-old's wages for male senior high school graduates.
(3)(c) Severance payment for senior high school graduates whose job tenures are 35 years.
(4) Figures in parentheses are the asymptotic t-ratios.
(5) * implies statistical significance at the 0.10 level, and ** at the 0.05 level.

that several variables have common effects (i.e., either positive or negative) on the rate of separations. Specifically, the wage profile, which is given by the growth rate of wages from 30-years-old to 45-years-old, has significant negative effects in both union firms and non-union firms. The steeper the wage profile, the lower the rate of separation. Regular working hours have significant positive effects in both union firms and non-union firms. This is somewhat counter-intuitive. The days of paid holidays are consistent with intuition because they have negative effects with statistical significance. Several other variables such as firm size and specific human capital accumulation are likely to have an influence on the rate of separations. Sales per employee and wage profile can be regarded as the proxies for these variables.

The fact that the voice of employees in union firms lowers the rate of employee separations suggests that firm-specific human capital investment in union firms is common and abundant. If this were true, it would imply that the effect of job tenure on wages is larger in union firms than in non-union firms. It is appealing to inquire whether or not the above statement is supported by data. Since our data do not have sufficient information on job tenure, we are unable to examine it. See Noda (1997b) on this.

6.3.5 Summary

It would be useful to provide our interpretation of the finding on no effect on wages, and the positive effect on several working conditions and the rate of separations. Long-term employment has been a social norm for the majority of both employers and employees in Japan. Thus, employees are not concerned so much with the short-run benefit such as wage payments but with the long-run benefit such as severance payment, internal career, and long-run prosperity of firm. If an increase in wages hurts firm's performance, and thus growth of firm, the long-run perspective is likely to be sacrificed. Since unions are interested in the long-run perspective of their firm, employees do not demand extremely high wages, and try to stay longer in the firm. These description may be called a cooperative behaviour based on the preference for the long-run perspective of both employers and employees (or unions).

In summarizing this section, it is concluded that the voice of employees in union firms not only reduces the rate of separations through the intermediary and indirect effect on the increase in the amount of severance payments and/or the reduction in regular working hours, but also reduces the rate of separations through the direct effect of employees' satisfaction. Employers can enjoy this benefit because they are able to collect returns on specific human capital investment such as training. This is true also for employees. The reason is that they would lose future wage growth if they separated from the firm in their early careers. The conclusion was obtained by the model which corrects a sample selection bias, and takes account of the effect of the voices of employees.

6.4 Concluding remarks

This chapter investigated the effect of unions on both wages and non-wage labour conditions, and separation rate in Japan. One important concern is the effect of the voices (or the bargaining powers) of employees on wages and non-wage labour conditions as the intermediary variable. Emphasis was placed on the difference between union firms and non-union firms with respect to the effect of the voices of employees. Several labour conditions which were examined are working hours, severance payment, paid holidays, the rate of paid holidays, overtime working hours, and the rate of separations in labour turnover.

We found the following results. First, the union endogeneity problem and/or selection problem is not so serious in Japan. Thus, we can estimate the effect of unions safely on the basis of ordinary least squares. The result is consistent with Freeman (1984) who does not denounce ordinary least squares. Second, we found that unions in Japan, on the one hand, had no effect on wages, and, on the other hand, had some effect on several non-wage labour conditions such as regular working hours and severance payments. Third, although there is no significant difference between union firms and non-union firms regarding monthly wage payments, the effect of working hours on per-hour wages is stronger in the former than in the latter. Thus, Japanese unions raise wages significantly by reducing regular working hours. Fourth, there are significant differences between union firms and non-union firms regarding the effect of the voices (or the bargaining powers) of employees. More specifically, union firms have a stronger influence on the voices than non-union firms. It is conjectured that some non-wage working conditions cannot be protected by informal associations such as employee associations. Formal unions rather than employee associations would be preferable for these fields. However, we find several labour conditions which do not show any differences between union firms and non-union firms regarding the effect of the voices of employees. Several economic interpretations, like the preference for long-term employment, and cooperative behaviour by both employers and employers, are provided to explain these results.

7
The Effect of Voices on Working Conditions and Their Economic Interpretation Based on Enterprise Unionism

7.1 Introduction

The previous chapter examined the effect of unions and employee voices on various working conditions, and attempted to test whether or not an endogeneity problem was serious. This chapter extends it in the following ways.

First, although an endogeneity problem (i.e., the joint determination of unions and their effect) was found to be unimportant, it would be necessary to take into consideration another kind of endogeneity issue when an intermediary variable, i.e., employee voices in this study, is included explicitly. We construct a recursive model to investigate the effect of unions on various working conditions. A recursive model intends to examine causality relationships both from trade unions to employee voices, and from employee voices to various working conditions.

Second, this chapter discusses the empirical result regarding the effect of trade unions based on the concept of enterprise unionism. Previously, we presented several evidences which support the fact that trade unions in Japan are enterprise unionism. Since no serious economic interpretations were provided, this chapter intends to make such an effort to prove that the interpretation based on enterprise unionism is relevant.

More concretely speaking, 'enterprise unionism' was believed to be one of the sources of a relatively better performance of firms in Japan because it encourages a cooperative behaviour of unions towards management. In other words, unions do not prefer an adversarial attitude, but want to work in close cooperation with management because they believe that the cooperative attitude produces an ultimate benefit to them. A more direct interest in the overall performance of the firm is ultimately more beneficial to employees than adversarial behaviour. The purpose of this study is to investigate whether or not there really is a non-adversarial attitude, and at the same time whether it contributes to the better performance of a firm.

The third subject which we would like to analyze is whether unions still stick to the principle of egalitarianism towards their members in the determination of wage and promotion. Egalitarianism here implies the following two characteristics. First, a wider wage distribution is not observed, but a more narrow distribution in wage payments and a more narrow assessment of individual employee performance are observed. Second, promotion to higher positions is not considered at earlier stages, but at relatively later stages. Also, it is determined on the basis of employees' seniority at least to certain levels rather than on the basis of assessment of individual employee performance. This can be tested by examining whether management's assessment of employee performance is approved by unions. We apply quantitative methods to investigate these subjects.

7.2 Enterprise unionism and labour participation

Chapter 2 explained very briefly enterprise unionism in Japan. This section discusses it fairly extensively.

There is a significant difference between Japan and Euro-American countries regarding the structure of unionism. While crafts unions and/or industrial unions, whose members consist of workers who engage in the same occupation and/or work in the same industry, are common in Europe and North America, enterprise unionism is quite common in Japan. Thus, it is important to discuss why and how enterprise unionism differs from craft unionism and/or industrial unionism, and several economic and social characteristics of unionism in Japan.

Enterprise unionism implies that employees in one firm organize their own union based on their initiative. All employees who are not on the management side and who are permanent regular workers in the firm can participate in the union, although some differences appear between closed-shops and open shops. About 90 per cent of unions are closed-shops. Thus, it is true that union membership is virtually compulsory if there is a union. 'All' means that there is no segregation by occupation regarding participation in the union. Blue-collar workers, white-collar workers, and sales workers join one union within the firm, although a substantial portion of white-collar employees who are promoted to managerial level leave the union in the middle of their careers because they are regarded as representing an employer side. In other words, union members are organized across all occupations, and thus special interests peculiar to particular occupations are not emphasized, although it happens occasionally that there is conflict among various occupations within one firm *vis-à-vis* an employer and/or management side. This implies that negotiation or collective-bargaining between an employer and employees is held between the representative of employers and the representative of employees within one firm, and thus nearly all decisions are made with the agreement of both sides with respect to wage determination and other working conditions. *Shunto* (annual spring offensive for wage bargaining) is one of the representative examples of the feature of enterprise unionism. See, for example, Gordon (1982) about *Shunto*.

Enterprise unionism does not necessarily imply, however, that all union movements are accomplished at the enterprise level. There is an upper-level organization at the industry level, say electric industry, banking industry, etc. The representative members from enterprise union members form an upper-level council, and they sometimes exchange information within the industry and discuss their view *vis-à-vis* the representative of employees in the industry. Two examples of their tasks are (1) upper-level wage bargaining at *Shunto* between employers and unions within the industry, which determines the average annual wage increase for the industry, and (2) determination of strike activity within the industry. These two examples suggest that industrial unions play some role even in Japan. However, the final and fundamental determination regarding wages and strike activity is made within the enterprise union, although it receives some consultation and suggestion from such an upper-level industrial union council.

Centralized union organizations such as LO and SAF in Sweden, and metal unions in Germany have stronger powers as centralized collective bargaining units than their Japanese counter-parts. See, for example, Calmfors and Driffil (1988), Calmfors (1993), Moene, Wallerstein and Hoel (1993), and Freeman and Gibbons (1995) about the implication of centralized collective bargaining units, and their time-series change in Sweden and other countries. It is shown that centralized wage setting is in a decreasing trend even in Sweden. Enterprise unionism in Japan can be understood as a decentralized collective bargaining unit in contrast to a centralized one. However, as will be explained later, the Japanese type of decentralized collective bargaining structure is quite different from that of the US, which is famous for another decentralized type, because wage determination of employees – in particular, white-collar workers – is on a fairly individual basis in the US, while it is not so strict in Japan even for white-collar workers.

One crucial issue is to examine the degree of tightness in the constraints imposed at the enterprise level after the industrial-level negotiation. Our understanding is that there is neither strict binding nor constraint at the enterprise level. There are three examples to support this. The first is that the industrial-level negotiation permits different levels of wage determinations among enterprises in the industry. Plausible empirical evidence supporting this contention is the fact that the variance of wages across firms within the same industry is different in Japan. See, for example, Nakata (1995) and Tachibanaki (1996a). The second is that there are always several enterprises which do not obey a strike order from the upper industrial-level union. The third is that matters associated with many kinds of working conditions other than wages at *Shunto* are negotiated at the enterprise level. In sum, the role of upper-level organization (i.e., industrial level or national level) is to provide only guidelines for enterprise bargaining, and not to give strong constraint on enterprise union activity.

It is possible to argue possible merits and demerits of both enterprise unionism, and crafts and/or industrial unionism. They are very brief to save space because this chapter discusses Japan almost exclusively. See Tachibanaki and Noda (1996) for the details. The merits of enterprise unionism are that both employers and employees can discuss the matters associated with their particular firm directly. Thus, they can be cooperative if everything goes well, and resolutions can reflect the performance of their firm. The merits of crafts unions are that the opinion or demand of employees who engage in a particular occupation can be expressed easily and their solidarity can be stronger. The merits of industrial unions are that there are extremely large numbers of union members, and thus the power can be stronger. The demerit of each union can be proposed easily, by considering the other side of the coin (the merit) which was explained here. For example, conflicts among different occupations in one firm can occur in enterprise unionism. Management has to negotiate with many unions in one firm in crafts unions. Individual enterprise performance cannot be taken into account seriously during a high level negotiation in industrial unions.

7.3 Voices of unions (employees) and management policies

There are various views about the relationship between management and unions. Two extremes may be described as follows. On the one hand, management should not be interfered with by unions in any field, but should have the 'right to manage'. On the other hand, management and unions should determine the fundamental principle together. This is the idea of 'co-determination', or 'participation of unions in management'. The first is common in many firms in the US, while the second is fairly common in many firms in Germany. In reality, some intermediary positions between the above two extremes are common in many firms in market economies, and this should be true even in the US and Germany.

Japanese firms have a somewhat peculiar position in comparison with firms in the US and Germany. It is fairly safe to say that there are no firms which have 'co-determination' or 'participation of unions in management', while it is true that unions are considerably cooperative with management. Koike (1977), for example, emphasized – based on his extensive fieldwork – the importance of a trade union in helping productivity improvement at the shop-floor level. Better quality of product and lower cost in production process can be achieved through a cooperative attitude of union workers. Koike's main interest was blue-collar workers. This study attempts to include both white-collar and blue-collar employees, and evaluates it quantitatively.

Industrial relations as a whole have the following property. It is sometimes said that management in Japan listens to the demands by unions, and takes them into account in formulating its management policy. Unions do not take an adversarial position, for example strikes or absences, in exchange for favourable treatment by management, and thus workers have high incentives and motivation to work hard and improve productivity. See, for example, Ohtake and Tracy (1994) about a lower rate of strikes in Japan than in the US. Another typical example which is famous internationally is the quality control (QC) circle. It is a voluntary group activity among employees for producing better-quality goods and services.

One natural question can be addressed. If the above hypothesis were correct, it would be possible to conclude that unionized firms take account of the demand in various working conditions of workers more extensively than non-unionized firms. At the same time, productivity or firm's performance at unionized firms would be higher than non-unionized firms. This is an interesting hypothesis to be tested, and the present chapter undertakes such a test.

Labour economists in the UK and US were similarly interested in investigating the subject. It was investigated by using the production function approach adopted by Brown and Medoff (1978); whether or not unions raise productivity. After a large number of studies in this field were examined, it was concluded by Addison and Hirsch (1989) that the contention that unions, on average, significantly raise productivity cannot be sustained while empirical evidence is mixed. Booth (1995), however, concludes that unionization in both the UK and the US appears, on average, to have had a negative impact on productivity and productivity growth in the 1980s.

The 'exit-voice' approach advocated by Freeman (1980a), and Freeman and Medoff (1984) is one of the most important stimuli for better economic performance behind this debate. Basically, the 'exit-voice' approach proposes that unions lower the rate of employee turnover because better communication between management and unions is established, and thus grievance is handled more efficiently. It is possible to raise a selection bias problem in analysis of this type because unions are most visible in declining industries. We pointed out earlier that selection bias problems were not so important, at least in Japan.

It seems to us that, except for Chapter 6 of this book, no serious attempt has been made to quantify the influence of 'voice' of unions (or employees), and to investigate the effect of its quantified index on labour turnover or productivity. This study constructs an index which is able to indicate the power or voice of unions, or the voice of employees if no union exists in a firm, and uses its index in later sections. This index should be expressed in the simplest manner, but should represent the voice of employees comprehensively. The method of constructing such an index will be explained later. It is noted that the method to construct the index in this chapter is different from that in Chapter 6.

There have been very few studies which investigate the effect of unions based on the voice approach in Japan as described previously. One exception is Muramatsu (1984) who supported the basic proposition of Freeman and Medoff (1984). His pioneering study, however, had two shortcomings. The first one is that the data applied by Muramatsu did not distinguish between unionized firms and non-unionized firms, but considered only the extent of union participation rates. Although the union density is not entirely useless, it obscures the effect of union versus non-union firms to a certain extent. Second, the union density is positively correlated with the size of firms in Japan, as was proposed previously. Unless the effect of the firm size is removed, it is likely that a spurious positive correlation between unions and productivity is observed because there is a general understanding that larger firms perform relatively better in many economic variables, including higher wage payments, in comparison with smaller firms.

See, for example, Ishikawa (1982) and Tachibanaki (1982, 1996a). Although the data used by Muramatsu did not enable him to remove the effect of the firm size, it is certainly desirable to do so. Since individual survey data are available, the above shortcomings can be overcome to a certain extent.

There is a common understanding that unions in Euro-American countries did not approve management's assessment of employee performance, and thus they demanded equal treatment and promotion among union members. This practice is true in particular among blue-collar workers. This is an Euro-American-type egalitarianism of unions towards their members. See, for example, Freeman (1980b, 1982). White-collar workers are apparently excluded from this practice. Ishida (1990) found through his extensive fieldwork and interviews that employees in Japan, and even blue-collar workers, did not reject management's assessment of individual employee performance, unlike Euro-American blue-collar employees. He proposed that unions and employees, in particular blue-collar workers, were willing to compete among them. In other words, Japanese employees did not stick to egalitarianism among employees or union members. It is possible to guess that this provided higher incentives of intense competition for promotion and wage. It is appealing to inquire whether or not the data support such a hypothesis.

In sum, we want to test the following hypothesis in this chapter for the effect of enterprise unionism in Japan. The principal motivation is that unions in Japan are cooperative in general because of enterprise unionism. This cooperative feature towards management is likely to raise productivity through various channels or causal relationships. The first channel is the effect of unions on the 'voice' of employees. One hypothesis to be tested is that higher voices of employees may improve the working conditions of employees. The second hypothesis is that they may affect the fundamental management policies such as assessment of worker performance and promotion of employees. The third hypothesis is that the combined effect of the previous two effects (i.e., hypotheses) may raise productivity. Besides these three hypotheses, we are also interested in whether or not unions stick to egalitarianism towards their members.

7.4 Data sources and preliminary analysis

We use the data source which was used in Chapter 5. See that chapter for the detail. We use another source of data called *Human Resource*

Management, Wage Determination and Industrial Relations at the latter part of Section 7.5, which presents and discusses a recursive type model. This recursive model includes the effect of 'voices' of employees as an endogenous variable. This data which was collected in 1991 has 195 firms in the Kansai area, the second largest metropolitan area in the west which includes Osaka, Kyoto and Kobe, and the distribution of unionized firms and non-unionized firms is 75.1 per cent versus 24.9 per cent. There is a slight over-representation of unionized firms in this data source. Since Ishida (1992) explained this data source extensively, we avoid repetition. Another reason for avoiding detailed explanation is that we use this source only as a minor and supplementary source.

Several preliminary statistical analyses for the main data source are performed to understand how data report on the difference between union firms and non-union firms. Table 7.1 shows a comparison between unionized firms and non-unionized firms on the average figures of several labour and working conditions, and variables related to management. The questionnaire prepared four choices for each question regarding various labour conditions and management variables, and firms chose one among these four choices. Quantification was made as follows. (i) No consultation with unions (or employees if no union is organized) is made. Thus, management can determine it exclusively. The value zero is assigned in this case. (ii) Unions (or employees) do not express their demand and opinion explicitly. Thus, management can determine it fairly exclusively. The value one is assigned. (iii) Unions (or employees) can express their demand and opinions fairly extensively. Thus, management takes account of them fairly seriously. The value two is assigned. (iv) Unions (or employees) can express their demand and opinions strongly. Thus, management takes account of them explicitly. The value three is assigned to represent this case.

Table 7.1 presents the average figures for unionized firms and non-unionized firms on each item, and the estimated t-values for the purpose of statistical testing of equality between two sample averages. The table indicates that unionized firms have higher average values than non-unionized firms for all the labour conditions and management variables. In other words, employees in unionized firms express their demands and opinions to the management side more strongly than those in non-unionized firms. Among many variables the four variables, namely (1) wage and bonus payment, (2) improvement in daily management matters, (3) fringe benefit, and (4) holiday and working

Table 7.1 Comparison of average figures between unionized firms and non-unionized firms on labour conditions and management variables

	Unionized	*Non-unionized*	*t-value*
Education and training	1.533	1.52	−0.219
Wage and bonus payment	2.494	1.151	−9.578
Improvement in daily management matters	2.044	2.018	−0.336
Fringe benefit	2.147	1.890	−3.200
Holiday and working hours	2.410	1.737	−7.092
Mandatory retirement and employment of older workers	1.741	1.018	−7.023
Worker re-allocation and transfer	1.494	1.292	−1.783
Management principle, and production and sales planning	1.432	1.384	−0.414

Notes: Each labour condition or management condition is scaled by zero, one, two, or four. Value zero signifies no consultation with unions (or employees), while value four signifies strong demand by unions (or employees) is expressed. Thus, the higher the figure in this table, the stronger unions' (or employees') demand and consultation. The result in this table is somewhat different from that in Table 6.4 because of the difference in the sample size.
Source: RIALS, *Expectation and Effect of Trade Unions*, 1991.

hours, show higher values (i.e., over 2.0) in unionized firms. They imply that employees can express their demands and opinions fairly extensively, and that management takes account of them fairly seriously. Incidentally, the three variables, namely (1) wage and bonus payment, (2) holiday and working hours, and (3) mandatory retirement and employment of older workers, show the largest difference between unionized firms and non-unionized firms in view of the *t*-value test statistics. Unions are most effective in these variables.

It must be noted, nevertheless, that the other three variables, namely (1) education and training, (2) worker re-allocation and transfer, and (3) management principle, and production and sales planning, do not show such high values (say between 1.0 and 2.0) even for unionized firms. The implicaiton is somewhere between 'do not express explicitly' and 'can express fairly extensively'. Equivalently, the difference between unionized firms and non-unionized firms is small in these variables in view of the t-value statistics. These labour conditions and management variables can be regarded as the fundamental management policy which determines the general management course or the highest level management activity of the firm, and thus the management side interprets that fundamental policy must be determined by the management side without any serious consultation with employees. These variables are the symbol of 'right to manage'.

Based on the result in Table 7.1, it is possible to conclude that employees in unionized firms can express their demands and opinions to management more strongly than those in non-unionized firms for the matters which are directly related to employees' working conditions such as wages, working hours, fringe benefits, shop floor and office daily matters. On more fundamental management matters, however, there is little consultation with employees, and the management side determines them almost exclusively. Some readers may understand that the latter property is natural because 'right to manage' is a fundamental rule in any capitalist country, while some other readers may say that it is caused by the limitation of trade union movements, and at the same time that the system of co-determination, or labour-managed firm, is desirable. Although this is an appealing subject, it goes beyond the scope of this chapter.

7.5 The effect on productivity

This section presents the estimated result on the effect of unions on productivity. We use two different approaches to investigate this issue. The first is to use the ordered probit estimation method, and the second is to use a recursive model with two-stage least squares method. The first method applies a single equation model, while the second method uses the 'voice' variable as an endogenous intermediary variable between employees and productivity. We explained the meaning of the 'voice' of employees, which can be interpreted as a variable representing the negotiation power of employees on various management matters and labour conditions. Since this variable has never been quantified, we would like to do so, and to use it as an explicit endogenous intermediary variable.

'What kind of variable is used to represent productivity?' is a controversial subject in this literature. We take the per-capita sales variable to indicate productivity, mainly because this variable is the most reliable in this data source. It may be useful to state that this variable is accepted in many studies, as well as value-added, as given by Addison and Hirsch (1989), and Booth (1995).

Two reservations are described regarding sales values. The first is that the change in the macroeconomic environment is not taken into account. The second is that it is desirable to take account of the demand side for sales. Since this study applies a common period for measurement, i.e., the past five years, we assume that any change in the macroeconomic environment had an equal impact on all firms. Thus, the first reservation is not so serious, as it appears. The same answer can be given to the second reservation. However, the demand differs considerably from industry to industry even within the same year. Therefore, the second reservation is more serious than the first one, and it would be desirable to estimate our model for each industry separately. Alternatively, it would be desirable to construct a simultaneous equation model which takes into consideration the effect of demands.

The first result is presented here. The dependent variable is measured by the growth rate of per-capita sales values compared with that of five years ago. There are five choices for this variable. The value four indicates large increase, three indicates small increase, two indicates no change, one indicates small decrease, and zero indicates large decrease. It was found that statistical testing based on the estimated *t*-values whether or not there was a difference between unionized firms and non-unionized firms regarding the growth rate of sales values suggested no difference at all.

It is not surprising to find that there has been no difference between unionized firms and non-unionized firms regarding the growth rate of sales values because this variable is influenced by many other variables to a large extent. Our main concern is to investigate the following question: 'What variables are influential on the determination of the growth of sales, and at the same time, are there any differences between unionized firms and non-unionized firms regarding the effect of these variables?' Therefore, we estimated the growth of sales value equation separately between unionized firms and non-unionized firms by adopting the common independent variables, and examined the effect separately.

Table 7.2 shows the estimated result based on the ordered probit method. This estimation method is suitable for data with a categorized and discretely-ordered nature. Quantification of the independent variable is the same as the one given in Table 7.1. This table suggests the following observations. First, there are several variables which have positive effects on the growth of sales with statistical significance for unionized firms. They are (1) wage and bonus, and (2) management principle, and production and sales planning. If the degree of consultation with employees (or unions) for the above matters were higher, the growth rate of sales would be higher. Productivity is likely to be influenced positively in unionized firms when these variables (or matters) are handled properly between management and union. It is interesting to note that these two variables are not statistically significant in non-unionized firms. Previously, we found that a variable such as management principle, and production and sales planning, did not differ significantly between unionized firms and non-unionized firms in Table 7.1. This previous result is not inconsistent with the finding in Table 7.2, because the result in Table 7.2 shows separate data for unionized firms and non-unionized firms.

Second, other variables such as (1) workers' re-allocation and transfer, and (2) labour separation rate, are negatively significant. The first variable is somewhat surprising because it may imply that more

Table 7.2 The effect of various variables on the growth rate of per-capita sales (i.e., productivity) for the 'RIALS data'

	Unionized	*Non-unionized*
Wage and bonus	0.245*	−0.001
	(1.824)	(0.012)
Improvement in daily matters	−0.172	0.286**
	(1.184)	(1.998)
Retirement and employment	−0.147	−0.071
	(1.152)	(0.591)
Transfer and re-allocation	−0.191	0.025
	(1.650)	(0.248)
Management principle, production and sales planning	0.257**	−0.052
	(2.329)	(0.046)
Separation rate	−0.044**	−0.414
	(2.613)	(0.393)
Firm size	0.403**	0.050**
	(2.338)	(1.999)
Job tenure	−0.009	−0.005**
	(0.910)	(2.068)
Male–female ratio	−0.028**	−0.002
	(2.253)	(0.184)
Log of likelihood	−189.96	−211.09

Notes: (1) Figures in parentheses are the asymptotic t-ratios.
(2)* implies statisitical significance at the 0.1 level, and ** at the 0.05 level.

consultation on transfer of human resources within the firm is likely to give a negative effect on productivity. It should be understood that more consultation with unions on this matter is likely to encourage the firm to allocate human resources and employees more efficiently because a union worked as a barrier to efficient human resource allocation. Our result is a puzzle. Alternatively, it should be possible to propose that less consultation with unions on this matter provides better allocation of human resources within the firm. The second variable, namely the effect of labour separation rate, is quite understandable in view of the fact that the lower the separation rate, the higher the skill level in the firm. Firm-specific human capital is kept, and even increases, when employees stay longer in the firm. See these arguments in Benson (1994), Brunello (1992), Morishima (1991a, b and 1992) and Muramatsu (1984) who proposed the importance of firm-specific human capital, skill and training accumulated in the firm. Both firms and unions are willing to share rent yielded by capital and skill. It is noted that all these studies do not necessarily support the effect of unions on productively positively. They refer to the importance of training and specific capital in Japan by and large. Lower turnover rates support it strongly. See a work by Noda (1997a) who estimated the difference between unionized firms and non-unionized firms regarding the effect of firm-specific human capital.

Next, the second result is presented. Table 7.3 shows the estimated result whose model is given by the recursive type simultaneous equations described below,

$$VOICE = f\,(UNION, \text{Exogenous variables}) + u_1$$
$$EFFECT = g\,(VOICE, \text{Exogenous variables}) + u_2$$

where *VOICE* denotes the degree of negotiation power of employees, *EFFECT* denotes the variable concerned such as productivity, *UNION* denotes a union dummy, and u_1 and u_2 are error terms. The *VOICE* variable has been constructed in the following way. We considered six variables representing the various labour conditions. Each firm was asked to evaluate the degree of consultation between an employer and employees for each labour condition, and to choose one answer among the four alternative answers from the highest consultation to the lowest consultation. The principal component analysis was used to represent the overall degree of the 'voice' based on the above six variables.

It would be useful to describe the reason for introducing a recursive type simulaneous equations model here. The idea is that first, the VOICE equation is explained by both UNION and Exogenous variables,

Table 7.3 Estimated results of the effect of 'voices' on per-capita sales (i.e., productivity) for the 'human resource management' data

Dependent/ Independent	*Per-capita sales (log form)*
Constant	9.811**
	(2.318)
Age	−0.144
	(1.584)
Education	0.015
	(1.611)
Female	−0.001
	(0.127)
Size (dummy)	−0.980
	(1.194)
Industry (dummy)	−1.322
	(2.231)
Voice	1.659*
	(1.875)
S.E.	1.212
Estimation	2SLS

Notes: (1) Figures in parentheses are the asymptotic *t*-ratios.
(2) *implies statisitical significance at the 0.1 level, and ** at the 0.05 level.
(3) The meanings of the variables are as follows. Age is the average age of employees. Education is the average educational attainment of employees. Sales is the firm's per-capita sales value. It is given by the log-form. Females is the rate of female employees in a firm. Size is a dummy variable for the size of firm; unity if the number of employees is greater than 300 and zero otherwise. Industry is a dummy variable; unity if manufacturing and zero if non manufacturing.

and second, the EFFECT equation is explained by both the predetermined VOICE and Exogenous variables. The simple causality proceeds in the following way, namely UNION → VOICE → EFFECT. UNION affects VOICE, first, and then VOICE affects EFFECT. A possible outcome anticipates that unions may raise the negotiation power of employees, and then the higher negotiation power may raise the working conditions of employees. A recursive simultanous equations model fits well in order to examine this type of recursive causation.

It should be emphasized that the data source in this second model is different from the main data used in this chapter. Also, the dependent variable is not the growth of sales but the level of per-capita sales. As will be explained later for the UK studies, the estimated result is different between growth and level, because growth includes the effect of the time-series changes. The data section explained the source, and presented several brief statistical results of this source called *Human Resource Management, Wage Determination and Industrial Relations*. Thus, the estimated result is examined directly.

Since we are concerned only with the effect of the 'voice' of employees, i.e., the negotiation power of employees, only the result on the second equation is presented in Table 7.3. It shows that the effect of the 'voices' is positive, and statistically significant. Thus, the influence of the 'voice' works fairly favourably to raise per-capita sales value and thus productivity. Since the OLS result, which was estimated preliminarily and is not presented here to save space, showed a statistically insignificant coefficient of the 'voice' in the per-capita sales equation, the joint determination of productivity and 'voice', i.e., the recursive type simultaneous equations model, is a significant improvement in view of the statistically significant coefficient of the 'voice' estimated by the 2SLS in Table 7.3. Simply, the 2SLS result is superior to the OLS result. The result in this table is fairly consistent with Table 7.2 in the sense that the negotiation power supported by a trade union raises productivity.

The two data sources examined above support the view that unions in Japan are likely to raise productivity, and confirms an early study by Muramatsu (1984), and a recent study by Noda (1997a). Benson (1994), however, has a different opinion for manufacturing industries. This seems to be a big contrast with the US evidence that unions do not on average significantly increase productivity. See Booth (1995) on this. The UK evidence is mixed, as surveyed by Booth (1995), and Metcalf (1989, 1993). The British evidence suggests that nearly all studies report a negative impact on the level of productivity. However, it proposes that unionization in Japan had a significant positive impact on productivity growth in the 1980s because of weakening trade union power and anti-union legislation. The Japanese case estimated here suggests that both the level and the growth produced the similar implication.

Why is there such a difference between Japan and the Anglo-Saxon countries? According to our judgment one of the most important causes lies in the fact that Japan has the so-called enterprise unionism. Section 7.7 evaluates the importance of enterprise unionism.

7.6 The effect of voices on wage increases and bonuses: the RIALS data

This section reports some results of the estimated functions for wage increases and bonus payments which are explained by the influence of 'voices' and some other exogenous variables. The data source is the 'RIALS data', as was explained previously. This data source was analyzed by Tachibanaki and Noda (1993) extensively, and in the previous section. Thus, this section presents only the relevant part which is strictly related to the subject of this study, namely the effect of 'voices' on assessment of individual employee performance.

The model in this section is similar to the previous recursive model:

$$VOICE = f\,(UNION, \text{Exogenous Variables}\,) + u_1$$
$$ASS = g\,(VOICE, \text{Exogenous Variables}\,) + u_2$$

where *VOICE* denotes the extent of the voices of employees, *UNION* denotes a union dummy and *ASS* denotes the respective dependent variable such as (Regular) Wage Increase, (2) Bonus Payments, and (3) Age at which promotion is determined.

It is necessary to explain how these dependent variables, except for (3) Age, are quantified. The question asks the extent of the regular wage increases and the bonus payments judged by individual employee performance. The former is classified as follows: (1) within 10 per cent above or below the average increase in wages, (2) between 11 and 20 per cent, (3) between 21 and 30 per cent, (4) between 31 and 40 per cent, (5) between 41–50 per cent, (6) over 51 per cent. We assign the values of 5 to (1), 15 to (2), 25 to (3), 35 to (4), 45 to (5), and 55 to (6), respectively, in order to quantify the increase in regular wages based on the assessment of employee performance. The bonus payment is quantified in a similar way to the regular wage increase. Starting age of promotion needs no explanation because age can be used as the dependent variable directly.

The 'voice' variable is measured by the simple average of eight working conditions. Those eight conditions and variables are (1) training, (2) bonus and wage, (3) daily management matters, (4) fringe benefit, (5) holiday and working hours, (6) mandatory retirement, (7) transfer of employees in both section and establishment, and sending off to group companies, and (8) management principle, and production and sales planning at higher levels. Four different levels of answers were prepared to indicate the extent of the voices of employees for each question of the eight variables. The simple average is used as the actual

Table 7.4 Estimated results of the effect of 'voices' on the increase in wages and bonuses payments for the 'RIALS data'

Dependent/ Independent	*Voice*	*Increase in wages*	*Bonuses*
Constant	2.393**	−0.832	−0.435
	(8.190)	(0.064)	(0.035)
Union (dummy)	0.312**		
	(4.874)		
Age	−0.001	0.006	−0.0002
	(0.991)	(0.409)	(1.178)
Tenure	0.016**	−0.216	−0.268
	(1.991)	(0.896)	(1.217)
Size of firm	0.076**	0.955	1.591*
	(2.258)	(1.002)	(2.061)
Industry dummy (manufacturing)	0.071	1.534	1.315
	(1.216)	(1.050)	(0.971)
Regional dummy I	−0.034	0.838	−0.677
	(0.499)	(0.503)	(0.433)
Regional dummy II	−0.080	0.202	−1.590
	(0.996)	(0.105)	(0.855)
Regional dummy III	−0.125	1.988	0.016
	(1.456)	(0.932)	(0.309)
Log of per-capita sales	0.030	−2.270**	−1.314*
	(0.999)	(3.067)	(1.867)
Voice		5.293	5.060
		(1.085)	(1.178)
R^2 (adjusted)	0.156		
S.E.	0.558	13.30	12.60
Estimation	OLS	2SLS	2SLS

Notes: (1) Figures in parentheses are the asymptotic *t*-ratios.
(2) * implies statistical significance at the 0.1 level, and ** at the 0.05 level.
(3) The meanings of the variables are as follows. Tenure is the average tenure of employees. Size of firm is the log of employees. Union is a dummy variable. Sales is the firm's per-capita sales value. It is given by the log-form because it is used as the independent variable. Voice, increase in wages and bonuses were explained in the main text.

extent of the 'voice'. The higher the simple average is, the higher the 'voice' is.

Table 7.4 shows the estimated result for the regular wage increases, and the bonus payment, on the basis of the assessment of individual employee performance. The union dummy variable is positive with statistical significance. Thus, a union raises the negotiation power of employees significantly. An interesting result appears in the effect of 'voices' on the regular wage increases and the bonus payments. The 'voice' variables are not statistically significant for both equations. In other words, the "voices" of employees are not influential at all in the determining of both the regular wage increases and the bonus payments. The average value of the wage increase is 17.48 per cent for unionized firms and 15.86 per cent for non-unionized firms, and the average value of the bonus payment is 17.30 per cent for unionized firms, and 16.26 per cent for non-unionized firms. These two differences between unionized firms and non-unionized firms are not statistically significant according to the *t*-test. These results suggest that although a wider assessment is held for unionized firms than for non-unionized firms, the difference is not statistically significant. Accordingly, we may conclude that management can determine the extent of the regular wage increases and of the bonus payments for individual employees on the basis of the assessment of employee performance without consulting with employees. It does not necessarily imply, however, that employees have no influence on the determination of wages and bonuses. The average wages and bonuses of all employees are negotiated with employees in *Shunto*.

Table 7.5 shows the estimated result for promotion. The dependent variable is the starting age for promotion on the hierarchical ladder in a firm. Employees who are promoted and not promoted appear at this age. The result indicates the fact that the 'voice' variable is positive with rigorous statistical significance for both senior high school graduates and university graduates. Thus, the 'voices' of employees tend to postpone the starting age for promotion. Early promotion is not preferred because the 'voices' of employees are stronger. The average starting age of promotion for senior high school graduates is 33.25-years-old for unionized firms and 31.03-years-old for non-unionized firms, and it is 32.84-years-old for the former and 30.80-years-old for the latter for university graduates. It is found that these two differences between unionized firms and non-unionized firms are statistically significant according to the *t*-test. Therefore, we may conclude that unions try to postpone the starting age for promotion, and thus prefer egalitarianism at least with respect to promotion of employees. Egalitarianism here implies that promotion to higher positions is made at relatively late stages in an employee's career, unlike the US promotion system where promotion is made earlier for high-flyers who are very productive. It is noted, nevertheless, that unions tended to reduce wage dispersion even in the US, as given by Freeman (1980b, 1982), Hirsch (1982), and others. Egalitarianism can work in two different areas, namely promotion and wage dispersion.

Table 7.5 Estimated results of the effect of 'Voices' on the promotion for the 'RIALS data'

Dependent/ Independent	*Voice*	*Starting age of promotion (senior high)*	*Starting age of Promotion (university)*
Constant	2.453**	11.574**	12.475**
	(9.022)	(2.704)	(3.056)
Union (dummy)	0.276**		
	(4.389)		
Age	−0.001**	0.002**	0.018**
	(2.106)	(4.352)	(3.820)
Tenure	0.016**		
	(2.039)		
Size of firm	0.056*	−0.193	−0.177
	(1.816)	(0.580)	(0.547)
Industry dummy	−0.100*	−1.324**	−1.211*
(manufacturing)	(1.732)	(2.255)	(1.941)
Regional dummy I	0.012	0.552	0.701
	(0.183)	(0.838)	(1.129)
Regional dummy II	−0.018	1.039	1.019
	(0.230)	(1.377)	(1.407)
Regional dummy III	−0.119	0.787	0.821
	(1.466)	(0.962)	(1.037)
Log of per-capita sales		4.950**	5.003**
		(3.113)	(3.098)
Voice		4.950**	5.003**
		(3.113)	(3.098)
R^2 (adjusted)	0.156		
S.E.	0.563	5.631	5.228
Estimation	OLS	2SLS	2SLS

Notes: (1) Figures in parentheses are the asymptotic *t*-ratios.
(2) *implies statistical significance at the 0.1 level, and ** at the 0.05 level.
(3) The meanings of the variables are as follows. Tenure is the average tenure of employees. Size of firm is the log of employees. Union is a dummy variable. Sales is the firm's per-capita sales value. It is given by the log-form. Voice, increase in wages and bonuses were explained in the main text.

7.7 Overall evaluations

This chapter investigated the influence of unions in Japan on various economic variables by using two useful individual survey data. We gave a comprehensive examination for the first 'RIALS data' and a brief examination for the second 'Human Resource Data'. Since one of the reasons for the lack of studies on the relationship between unions and firms' performance was the data problem, this study shed light on the understanding of enterprise unionism in Japan.

There are several channels or causal relationships when we investigate the effect of unions on various economic variables such as productivity, wage dispersions, or others. The first channel is the effect of the existence of unions on the 'voice' of employees. There are many non-unionized firms in Japan. Thus, it is necessary to investigate whether or not there is a difference between unionized firms and non-unionized firms regarding the voice. A collective bargaining is normally held between the representative of the so-called 'enterprise union' (i.e., only one union in a firm, and all employees belong to this union) and the management side. If there is no union in a firm, there is usually some kind of employee association. Even if neither union nor employee association exists, some negotiations are still held between employers and employees.

We found the following results. First, the difference between unionized firms and non-unionized firms is significant in certain variables associated with the following working and labour conditions: (1) wage and bonus, (2) fringe benefit, (3) holiday and working conditions, (4) mandatory retirement and employment of older workers, and (5) improvement in daily management matters. Unions are likely to raise the negotiation power (i.e., the voice) for these variables. However, the fundamental management policy such as (1) training, (2) staffing rule (i.e., re-allocation of human resources within the firm), and (3) management principle, and production and sales planning, does not show any difference between them.

Second, productivity is increased when there is a trade union in a firm. This result was supported by the two data sources, and the positive effect on productivity was verified for both growth and level in sales values. It is quite likely that the negotiation power which may be called the 'voice' of employees, contributed to the positive effect on productivity. It was found that several variables such as (1) wage and bonus, and (2) management principle, and production and sales planning are effective in raising productivity among unionized firms, although on average unions do not have high negotiation powers in these variables in comparison with non-unionized firms.

The second channel is the effect of the 'voice' of employees on management policy. We considered two effects: (1) the management's assessment of individual employee performance for wage increase and bonus payment, (2) the determination of the starting age for promotion. We found the following two conclusions. First, there is no significant difference between unionized firms and non-unionized firms with respect to the extent the management's assessment of individual employees for wage increases and bonus payments. Second, there is some difference between unionized firms and non-unionized firms regarding the determination of the starting age for promotion. In sum, the management side is able to determine these matters almost exclusively without any consultations with unions or employees except for the determination of the starting age for promotion.

It is possible to point out three alternative reasons for this conclusion. The first is that unions or employees in Japan have abandoned the principle of egalitarianism, or have never held it. Therefore, they did not demand equal treatment of employees to the management side. The second is that the current assessment system is judged as fair by unions or employees. Thus, they accept the current status, and do not feel any dissatisfaction. The third is that management did not listen to the demands of unions or employees in assessing individual employees' performance and determining the wage level and the bonus level of employees. Management believes that these are at the discretion of management and are not to be interfered with by unions or employees.

It is impossible to select the most relevant reason among the above three alternative reasons in this study. We are inclined to believe that these three are equally important in explaining the reasons for our findings in this study, and that the Japanese industrial relations system has the optimum level or extent of management's assessment of individual employees and wage dispersion which is likely to satisfy both management and employees. This is a Japanese style of cooperative behaviour by both employers and employees. 'Enterprise unionism' is one of the backgrounds which support it institutionally. Future careful works are called for to confirm or reject our conjecture of the optimality. It should be pointed out, however, that there is one area in which unions demand equal treatment; that is promotion. Unions seem to be successful in postponing the starting age for promotion. This late promotion was also preferred by employers in order to give strong incentive to all employees in a firm. If early selections were made, employees who were not promoted would lose incentive. Late selections can induce higher incentive in all employees.

The final channel is the effect on productivity. The two results in Tables 7.2 and 7.3 showed that the 'voice' of employees, namely the negotiation power of employees, was influential in raising the per-capita sales value in a firm. The effect is statistically significant. Although this 'voice' may work in the opposite direction (i.e., a negative effect on productivity), the Japanese data showed a positive effect. Thus, we confirmed, by using the individual survey data, the findings of the pioneering work of Muramatsu (1984). The opposite direction may postulate, 'If management listened too much to the demands of employees, productivity would be lowered.' In this case, a higher management autonomy is preferable for productivity.

We have not given any conclusive discussions on the reasons for obtaining our result, although we have described them briefly. One plausible cause, which can be derived from our current study, is as follows. Management is able to manage a firm on the fundamental management issues without any serious interventions from unions or employees, although some degree of consultation in the field of working conditions such as wages, fringe benefit, and working hours, between employers and employees is likely to encourage higher productivity. Unions may be too quiet, and accept the management policies without strong opposition except for several fields associated with employees' working conditions listed above. In other words, unions do not oppose the fundamental management policy proposed by management, but demand only a limited field of working conditions from management. Since management is willing to accept such limited fields, unions (and thus employees) behave in a quite cooperative manner, and thus try to contribute to higher productivity of a firm in exchange for even such a limited degree of favourable treatment by an employer.

We can offer three alternative judgments about this interpretation. Some people may say that this is nothing but a cooperative behaviour of both management and unions (employees). Some people may say that Japanese management is superb, and Japanese unions (employees) are too weak. Some people may say that both Japanese management and unions (employees) are superb at least in raising productivity of their firm. It is necessary to investigate which of the above three different judgments is the right one. 'Enterprise unionism', which is different from crafts unionism or industry unionism in Euro-American countries, is likely to explain most of the above account.

Enterprise unionism, in fact, can support all the above three judgements in the following way. Unions or employees understand that too many demands to management, and an adversarial attitude towards management is detrimental for the firm because they are likely to reduce its competitive position in the industry. Competition among firms in one industry is obviously very severe. International competition also is acute recently. Employers also understand that it is crucial to provide their employees with a higher incentive to work hard and a lesser degree of hostile attitude, to raise productivity. Enterprise unionism operates fairly efficiently when both sides have common interests. We find that one of the common interests is to increase the competitive power of the firm (i.e., the growth of output, sales, or profit), and to believe that the fruits of the growth should be shared by both sides. Therefore, the two parties become cooperative. It is not a zero-sum game between the two parties, which seeks to maximize the share of a constant fruit. It is important to add the fact that unions are organized in larger firms in Japan, which have a relatively high competitive advantage in the industry. Thus, both parties could enjoy the above feature, possibly at the expense of smaller firms.

Cooperative behaviour of both employers and unions has worked well during the period of better macroeconomic performance, i.e., the growing economy. The future course of the Japanese economy is not so bright but fairly gloomy. It is an open question whether or not enterprise unionism operates and survives as it has in the past.

8
The Effect of Union Voices on Productivity

8.1 Introduction

This chapter investigates whether or not unions raise productivity through the voice of unions. In particular, we are concerned with union participation in management, information-sharing between management (i.e., firm) and unions, QC circles and some other forms. We examine whether these items contribute to increasing productivity in a firm. Chapter 7 investigated whether or not there is any difference between unionized firms and non-unionized firms regarding productivity. This chapter is concerned with the following institutional questions: whether or not participation of unions in management, and information-sharing between management and unions, are effective for raising management efficiency (i.e., productivity), given that unionized firms have higher productivity than non-unionized firms as was verified in Chapter 7. This chapter attempts to investigate the mechanism which produced such management efficiency, and the role of unions in this mechanism.

8.2 Participation of employees (unions) in management: voices and productivity

8.2.1 Better communication between management and employees

Japanese unions provide their voices not only on various working conditions such as wages, working hours, and some other working conditions, as Chapters 6 and 7 of this book have presented, but also various management matters. Management sides are willing to listen to unions' demand for general management matters. It is, however, an open question whether or not the management side modifies its top-level policy after listening to unions' demand.

We can cite two examples of management attitude towards unions' demand for involvement in top level policy. German firms have a tradition of co-determination between management and unions. Thus, Germany may be regarded as a country where unions' demand is discussed seriously with management, and top-level management policy reflects the demand and opinions of unions to a certain extent. The other extreme is the American case where firms do not listen to unions' demand for management policy. In other words, the management side and union side (or employees) are separated, and thus there is a consensus that the right of management should not be interfered with by anybody. What is the situation in Japan? This is the concern in this chapter.

We understand that Japanese management is willing to listen to unions' (or employees') demands, but whether or not the management side accepts them or modifies top management policy after consultation depends on the issue of top management policy, as Chapter 7 of this book presented. Other important characteristics which are emphasized in this chapter are as follows. First, unions are likely to modify their demands or even withdraw them altogether should they recognize that such demands might hurt the firm's business performance. Second, it is likely that both management and unions have a strong common incentive for increasing the competitive edge of their firm after they share common information on current management problems or the future course of their firm. Chapter 7 of this book described one interpretation regarding the second point; enterprise unionism in Japan can be a candidate for supporting it.

Communication between management and unions is held at various levels and about various issues. The highest level communication is between top management and top leader of unions with respect to the highest management matters such as general management strategy, wage determination at *Shunto*, possible negotiation on layoffs or discharges, etc. The middle level is concerned with job assignment, remuneration, working hours, general management and human resource management, etc. The shop-floor and office level is concerned with daily management matters, improvement in working conditions, operation assignment, etc. Kochan, Katz and McKersie (1986) considered the following three different levels for negotiations between management and unions (or employees): (1) the highest strategic level,

(2) the functional level, and (3) the shop-floor or office level. This chapter examines at what level communication between management and unions (employees) is held most efficiently, and in what way. At the same time, we examine whether or not such communication improves productivity or performance of a firm.

There are three channels which lead to increased productivity or performance when communication between management and unions (or employees) is held: in other words, unions' or employees' participation in management. First, it raises the loyalty of employees to the firm, and thus their work incentive. Second, information-sharing between management and employees improves management efficiency because each side (i.e., management or employees) can recognize the problems of the other side (i.e., employees or management) easily, and thus they can make a joint effort to solve these problems. Third, it is possible to raise the rate of return to firm-specific human capital, by having better communication between management and employees. When the rate of return to firm-specific human capital is increased, both management and employees can receive the benefit of such increase; improvement in productivity for the former, and higher wages for the latter.

8.2.2 Detailed discussions on the reasons for better performance

We would like to provide more detailed descriptions why the above three channels are useful to improve productivity or performance of a firm.

(1) Morishima (1991a,b) provided us with the relevant interpretation about the usefulness of information-sharing between management and employees. In particular, he emphasized the importance of management releasing information about the management and business conditions of the firm to employees, because it is likely that the management goal which aims at increasing management efficiency can be identified easily between the two sides, and both sides make a joint effort to achieve it.

Work councils, or joint labour–management conferences are the institutional systems which help both sides to have better communication or joint determination of management and employees at various levels and regarding various matters. Employees are able to recognize the importance of the relationship between the firm's performance and their work effort by information-sharing on business performance, financial conditions and human resource management programmes of the firm. Also, both management and employees can evaluate the role of human resource allocation within the firm jointly. These recognitions and evaluations are likely to increase the work incentive of employees, and thus productivity of the firm.

Employees' participation in management at the shop-floor or office level, such as QC circles (quality control circles) or frequent consultations and possible joint determination on team production, enables employees to feel that they are participating in management and to consolidate the solidarity between management and employees, and even among employees.

(2) Management can benefit by obtaining useful information on employees such as their attitude and demands in daily production and business activity. Also, managers and engineers can more effectively plan production or sales activity, or establish efficient production processes in the factory, when they know the capability and attitude of operators and manual workers. Lewin (1984), for example, raises the importance of communication between management and employees, in particular the management's knowledge on employees. Development of new products and new technology cannot be easily introduced and implemented in a production process without having the cooperative behaviour of workers in the factory. Such cooperative behaviour is intensified when information is shared, and communication takes place between management and employees frequently.

(3) The importance of firm-specific human capital investment can be recognized in relation to employees' participation into management.

At the firm level, it is anticipated that the introduction of a new product or a new technology in the production process will require a considerably drastic change in daily operation procedure and speed, and even in human resources allocation and skill level of employees. Therefore, re-training or a change in professional skill may be required to deal with such a drastic change. It is natural that information-sharing between management and employees on the firm's management policy and planning facilitates the implementation of such re-training and a change in human resources.

At the shop-floor or office level, we can point out that the importance of learning and training is crucial for producing better quality goods at cheaper prices. Management skill and efficient production processes are achieved when training and learning are organized and provided skillfully by the firm with the consent of employees, including job rotations within a firm or establishment and information-sharing on team production.

Firm-specific human capital is not only useful for the production process, but also for customer relations and human network in the firm. Good customer relations can be achieved when sales persons, or even production workers, including engineers, know the quality and characteristics of their products and technology in the house well. A good human network among managers and employees within the firm also enhances efficient production. They are the examples of the usefulness of firm-specific human capital.

Good communication between management and employees, and employees' participation into management can increase the rate of return of firm-specific human capital when both management and employees share information on the firm's business condition, products and technology. It is acknowledged that QC circles and team production work well in Japan because views are exchanged frequently and frankly. As Hashimoto (1990) notes, these practices enhance efficiency in management. If there is no serious communication between management and employees, or if some adversarial relationship between them is observed, then efficient management and less costly production processes are not achieved. The argument on the exit-voice approach in terms of Freeman and Medoff (1984) is also useful here.

Lewin (1984) identified four elements or conditions which would raise productivity or performance of a firm when employees' participation in management is guaranteed. (1) A profit-sharing scheme is prepared. (2) There is an institutional guarantee of permanent employment. (3) Wage differentials among employees are small. (4) Rights of employees are assured by the law.

The above is a brief account of the reasons why better communication between management and employees through various channels enables the firm to improve productivity or performance. We would like to test below whether this is empirically supported. We examine it for listed firms and unlisted firms separately.

It is noted that this study adopts panel data, which are different from cross-section data. While the latter cannot remove the effect of sample selection bias which is caused by a correlation between the effect of firms and the effect of trade unions, the former can control for the effect of firms. In order words, cross-section data are likely to show us that productivity of firms with trade unions is high, but are unlikely to show that trade unions raise productivity. Panel data enable us to remove such a sample selection bias.

Another advantage in using panel data is that we can estimate the effect of labour quality, which is indicated by job tenure, age and female ratio, on productivity of firms. In other words, we can identify the effect of labour quality on productivity and the effect of trade unions on productivity separately. Moreover, it is possible to anticipate that trade unions encourage their members to stay longer in the firm, and thus that their skill level is higher in unionized firms than that in non-unionized firms because of their longer job tenure on average. This is another indirect effect of trade unions on higher productivity. In sum, panel data enable us to estimate these effects separately.

Another interesting variable is years of firm duration – simply, the age of a firm since its establishment. If a firm operated longer, the ratio of longer-job tenured workers would be higher. Therefore, productivity of such a firm would be higher. It is an interesting subject to inquire whether or not the above guess is true. We investigate this issue.

The female–male ratio (simply, female ratio) is a complicated variable. It is possible to believe that the rate of turnover is higher for females than for males for various reasons. Thus, it is likely that firms do not want to provide their female employees with training in fear of their future job-leaving. This lowers the average productivity of firms which employ a higher share of female workers. However, the other story may be possible; firms try to hire female employees, whose propensity to leave is lower, by selecting them carefully. In such a case productivity of these firms may be higher. We investigate these issues.

8.3 Listed firms

8.3.1 Data source and estimation method

This section explains the data source and estimation method. The principal data source is the Japan Economic Journal's *Company Data File* from 1992 to 1995. The data have, thus, a panel nature. The data source includes only listed firms. Among firms in the manufacturing industries we chose 404 firms based on a pure random selection. The number of unionized firms is 350, and that of non-unionized firms is 54. Thus, the rate of non-unionized firms is 13 per cent, which is somewhat higher than the national level for listed firms. Since employees in listed firms (i.e., large firms) tend to organize a union, the rate of non-unionized firms is quite low.

Table 8.1 shows the summary statistics for this data source. The dependent variable is measured by value-added (i.e., operating profit + labour cost + depreciation costs), or per-capita value-added (i.e., per employee value-added). The important difference between the data

Table 8.1 Summary statistics

	Unionized (350 × 4)		*Non-unionized (54 × 4)*	
	Mean	*SD*	*Mean*	*SD*
Value-added	34776	90375	14389	20649
Per employee value-added	10.91	3.29	11.95	7.18
Number of employees	2956	7660	1329	2033
Capital–labour ratio	12.91	8.33	14.04	8.60
Male average job tenure	16.24	3.77	11.24	3.73
Male average age	39.03	3.34	35.65	3.01
Female/male ratio	0.259	0.258	0.390	0.340
Years since establishment	50.32	13.46	37.55	12.34

Note: Value-added, capital–labour ratio, etc. are measured by one million yen.
Source: Derived from Japan Economic Journal, *Company Data File*.

source for listed firms and those for unlisted firms is that value-added is used for the former, rather than sales values, in order to indicate productivity or performance of a firm. It is noted that value-added per employee is, probably, the best measure to indicate productivity. Since productivity in other chapters and in unlisted firms in this chapter is measured by sales-values per employee, the result for listed firms which uses value-added per employee is somewhat more reliable.

Table 8.1 indicates the following observations. First, figures of both value-added and of the number of employees are larger in unionized firms than in non-unionized firms. Figures of per-capita value-added, however, and of capital–labour ratio are larger in non-unionized firms than in unionized firms. This result implies that there is a substantial number of non-unionized firms which are relatively large in size. Second, the average job tenure for male employees is longer in unionized firms than in non-unionized firms. This is true also for the average age. These results suggest that the rate of separation in unionized firms is smaller than in non-unionized firms. This is consistent with the common understanding in Japan. Third, the rate of female employees over total employment is higher in non-unionized firms than in unionized firms, implying that females participate less than men in unions, or that a union is not organized easily when the number of female employees is large.

8.3.2 Empirical results

We estimate the Trans-log type and the Cobb-Douglas type of production function to measure the effect of unions on productivity difference as indicated in equations (8.1) and (8.2). Since we apply four years' successive data, a random effect model is used.

$$\ln Y = \alpha_i + \alpha_1 \ln L_{it} + \alpha_2 \ln K_{it} + \alpha_3 \ln L^2{}_{it} + \alpha_4 \ln K^2{}_{it} + \alpha_5 \ln L_{it} {}^* \ln K_{it} + \alpha_6 Ten_{it} + \alpha_7 Union_{it} + \alpha_8 Fem_{it} + \alpha_9 Age_{it} + \alpha_{10} Fa_{it} \quad (8.1)$$

$$\ln Y/L = \beta_i + \beta_1 \ln L_{it} + \beta_2 \ln K/L_{it} + \beta_3 Ten_{it} + \beta_4 Union_{it} + \beta_5\ Fem_{it} + \beta_6\ Age_{it} + \alpha_{10}\ Fa_{it} \quad (8.2)$$

where

$\ln Y$: value-added
$\ln Y/L$: per-capita value-added
$\ln L$: labour input
$\ln K$: capital(i.e., tangible asset)
$\ln K/L$: capital–labour ratio
Union: a union dummy, 1: unionized, 0: otherwise
Ten: average job tenure of male employees
Age: average age of male employees
Fem: the rate of female employees over male employees
Fa: years since a firm was established
α_i and β_i signify *i*-th firm's peculiar effect, implying that α_i and β_i can show the difference in management capability, employee quality, and others among firms. The subscript *i* signifies firm, while the subscript *t* signifies time.

We give a few explanations about how we measured both independent variables and dependent variables. For the value of production, the value-added or the per-capita value-added is used. The log-form is, in fact, applied in the actual estimation. A book value of fixed asset is used to represent capital. Labour input is measured by the number of both male and female employees. Both value-added and capital are deflated by the wholesale price index for industrial products and by the wholesale price index for capital goods, respectively.

Table 8.2 shows the empirical result for the Trans-log type function. It is found that in equation (1) the union dummy variable is negative with statistical significance, implying that a union is likely to affect productivity of a firm negatively.

Equation (2) includes an interaction variable between union dummy and average job tenure. Although the union dummy variable is also negative, the interaction variable is positive with statistical significance. This signifies that as the average job tenure is longer, the positive effect of a union on productivity is stronger. Our calculation suggests that the effect of a union turns out to be positive when the

Table 8.2 Estimated results for trans-log type production function (1990–3)

	(1)	(2)	(3)	(4)	(5)
lnL	0.834**	0.826**	0.937**	0.868**	0.808**
	(5.440)	(5.321)	(6.082)	(5.502)	(5.177)
ln*K*	0.021	0.024	0.057	−0.011	0.028
	(0.127)	(0.143)	(0.348)	(0.064)	(0.167)
lnL^2	0.068**	0.066**	0.068**	0.067**	0.067**
	(3.455)	(3.347)	(3.519)	(3.485)	(3.389)
lnK^2	0.050**	0.049**	0.053**	0.055**	0.048**
	(3.409)	(3.305)	(3.586)	(3.704)	(3.218)
ln*L* × ln*K*	−0.108**	−0.104**	−0.118**	−0.011**	−0.103**
	(3.655)	(3.523)	(4.022)	(3.852)	(3.477)
Union	−0.075*	−0.498**	−0.529**	0.200	−0.340**
	(1.744)	(3.376)	(3.171)	(0.323)	(2.687)
Ten	0.017	0.024	−0.013	−0.014	−0.007
	(0.356)	(1.337)	(1.520)	(0.545)	(0.871)
Fem	−0.031	−0.027	−0.875**	−0.040	−0.027
	(0.594)	(0.532)	(2.866)	(0.705)	(0.528)
Union × Ten		0.033**	0.027**	0.058**	0.022**
		(3.005)	(2.786)	(2.953)	(2.332)
Union × Fem			0.674**		
			(2.026)		
Ten × Size		0.003	0.003	0.003	0.003
		(1.292)	(1.357)	(1.143)	(1.487)
Age				0.129*	
				(1.730)	
Union × Age				−0.027	
				(1.258)	
Boom					0.088**
					(3.258)
Union × Boom					0.001
					(0.020)
Adj R^2	0.974	0.975	0.975	0.977	0.974
Hausman value	8.078	11.36	19.66	15.59	11.24
Probability	0.429	0.334	0.104	0.271	0.259

Notes: (1) Figures in parentheses are estimated *t*-values.
(2) * implies statistical significance at the 0.1 level, and ** at the 0.05 level.

average male job tenure is longer than 15.09 years. 64 per cent of our sample firms, in fact, show the positive effect. This figure is more than half, implying that many firms enjoy the positive effect of unions. We cannot, however, ignore the fact that the remaining firms have the negative effect of unions. The average male job tenure, namely 16.24 years, gives the positive effect of 3.8 per cent on productivity.

This value, i.e., 0.038, was obtained by the following equation: $\exp(-0.498+0.033 * 16.24)-1$, where -0.498 is the estimated coefficient for the union dummy and 0.033 is the estimated coefficient for the interaction variable.

It is possible to conjecture that the effect of firm-specific human capital is different by firm size. Thus, we added a firm size dummy (unity if the firm is larger than 1,000 employees, and zero otherwise) and its interaction with average job tenure. The result shows that the interaction coefficient is not statistically significant.

Equation (3) added an interaction variable between union dummy and the rate of female employees. The result shows that its coefficient is positive with statistical significance, implying that a union reduces the amount of the negative effect of the female ratio on productivity. The calculation suggests that the effect of a union is 4.4 per cent through its interaction with the female ratio.

Equation (4) takes into consideration both the effect of male average age and its interaction with union dummy. The coefficient of average age is positive, while its interaction is not statistically significant. We, thus, understand that the effect of age on productivity is not different between unionized firms and non-unionized firms.

Equation (5) adds both a boom dummy in the economy and its interaction. The estimated coefficients are not statistically significant. It may imply that the effect of unions on productivity for listed firms is unaffected by business cycles. We nevertheless need a more careful study which applies a longer period of data because the current study applies only four years' data.

Finally, it is noted that the estimated value of the Hausman statistics suggests support of the random effect model adopted in this study.

Next, we examine the estimated result based on the Cobb-Douglas type of production function and per-capita value-added as the dependent variable. Table 8.3 shows the result. We are able to conclude, based on this table, that the overall result is not different from that based on the Trans-log type. Thus, no interpretation of the result is provided.

We performed, nevertheless, several experiments in this table. First, equation (6) includes capital–labour ratio and its interaction with union dummy to examine whether or not the effect of capital–labour ratio is different between unionized firms and non-unionized firms. The estimated interaction coefficient is not statistically significant. Second, we also included the variable of years since establishment. It was not statistically significant. A similar story was true regarding the effect of working hours. Thus, they are not written here.

Table 8.3 Estimated results for Cobb-Douglas production function (1990–93)

	(1)	*(2)*	*(3)*	*(4)*	*(5)*	*(6)*
ln*L*	0.024**	0.009	0.021	0.010	0.009	0.008
	(1.800)	(0.492)	(1.092)	(0.539)	(0.451)	(0.429)
ln*K*/*L*	0.208*	0.205**	0.197**	0.211**	0.192**	0.169**
	(9.834)	(9.795)	(9.547)	(9.865)	(9.066)	(4.297)
Union	−0.087**	−0.549**	−0.614**	0.213	−0.357**	0.074**
	(2.020)	(3.714)	(3.452)	(0.347)	(2.790)	(0.119)
Ten	0.016	0.025	0.011	−0.001	−0.011	−0.001
	(0.356)	(1.381)	(0.645)	(0.039)	(1.311)	(0.083)
Fem	−0.039	−0.034	−0.709	−0.060	−0.029	−0.058
	(0.744)	(0.661)	(2.540)	(1.057)	(0.563)	(1.012)
Union × Ten		0.036**	0.036**	0.065**	0.023**	0.066**
		(3.268)	(3.238)	(3.365)	(2.400)	(3.432)
Union × Fem			0.510			
			(1.640)			
Ten × Size		0.003	0.009	0.003	0.014**	0.002
		(1.146)	(1.520)	(1.080)	(2.145)	(1.087)
Age				0.033*		0.034*
				(1.700)		(1.745)
Union × Age				−0.030		−0.031
				(1.428)		(1.466)
Boom					0.078**	
					(2.904)	
Union×Boom					0.009	
					(0.309)	
Union × *K*/*L*						0.063
						(1.352)
Adj R^2	0.672	0.672	0.674	0.691	0.671	0.690
Hausman value	8.977	10.24	23.64	13.07	12.31	11.51
Probability	0.110	0.175	0.014	0.159	0.100	0.318

Notes: (1) Figures in parentheses are estimated *t*-values.
(2) * implies statistical significance at the 0.1 level, and ** at the 0.05 level.

8.3.3 Economic interpretations

It is possible to conclude based on the result for listed firms that the effect of average male job tenure on productivity is positive for unionized firms, while we observe no effect for non-unionized firms. At the same time, the larger the share of employees with longer job tenures, the higher the productivity of a firm. Longer job tenures imply that they are highly experienced and skilled workers. A labour union lowers the degree of separations from the firm, and thus consolidates cooperative behaviour of both firm and employees. Such cooperative behaviour in unionized firms raises employees' work incentive, skill formation, and possibly solidarity, and thus loyalty to a firm as well as mutual trust.

When the average length of male job tenure is more than a certain critical number of years, the effect of a union on productivity turns out to be positive. It is recommended to keep longer-tenured employees in a firm to attain such a positive effect on productivity. Thus, a firm has to adopt a policy which prolongs job tenure of employees, and thus encourages them to stay in a firm. More concretely speaking, it is desirable to keep the optimum allocation between longer-tenured employees (i.e., skilled employees) and shorter-tenured employees (i.e., less-skilled employees).

It is possible to provide an alternative interpretation for our finding that the effect of job tenure on productivity is stronger in unionized firms than in non-unionized firms. Suppose that unionized firms are able to hire productive and capable workers more easily than non-unionized firms. In such a case the effect of job tenure on productivity would be stronger in unionized firms without manipulating the rate of return to job tenure. In reality, it is hard to believe that unionized firms in Japan are able to hire those workers in view of the fact that there is no significant difference in wage payments between unionized firms and non-unionized firms, provided that a firm with higher wage payments can hire a more productive worker. It is, nevertheless, important to add the fact that other working conditions, such as severance payments and working hours, are more favourable in unionized firms than in non-unionized firms despite no significant difference in wage payments between them, as shown in Chapters 5 and 6. This suggests that unionized firms can attract productive and capable workers more easily, and thus we believe that it is the real story.

After accepting that firms with unions are able to hire productive and capable workers more easily than those with no unions, it is possible to understand that the effect of job tenure is stronger in unionized firms. In terms of economics, we can say that these productive and capable workers are regarded as employees with higher trainability. The increase in productivity due to various training in a firm would be greater for employees with high trainability. It is hard to expect that unions are able to affect human capital investment directly. Therefore, it is reasonable to understand that unionized firms have a greater number of highly trainable workers than non-unionized firms. Since longer job tenures in these firms increase the rate of return to firm-specific training, the productivity in these firms can be higher.

As for the ratio of female to male employees, we found that unionized firms lowered the negative effect of the rate of female employees on productivity, although the effect of it in non-unionized firms was negative. It is possible to guess that more training is provided to female employees in unionized firms than in non-unionized firms.

The above two results, namely for both male and female employees, indicate the fact that unions are effective in raising the positive effect of firm-specific training through various channels, such as longer job tenures, etc., and thus they have a positive effect on productivity.

When the effect of average age on productivity was analyzed, we found no significant difference between unionized firms and non-unionized firms. If we were able to regard age as representing the general human capital, the result would imply that unions had not affected general human capital at all.

8.4 Unlisted firms

8.4.1 Data source and estimation method

This section explains the data source and estimation method. The principal source is the Japan Economic Journal's *Needs-Company Data File* from 1989 to 1995. This source consists of unlisted firms, and thus enables us to compare the previous result based on listed firms with that based on unlisted firms. Another important characteristic is the panel nature of the data (i.e., 1989–1995) which include both boom years and recession years in the Japanese economy.

The following four conditions were used to select firms for our investigation: (1) unlisted firms including counter-registered firms and counter-managed firms, (2) capitalization 30 million yen and over, (3) sales or business revenues 500 million yen and over, (4) both a balance sheet and a statement of profit and loss are reported. In addition to the above conditions we selected manufacturing firms randomly which reported firms' economic conditions during all seven years (i.e., 1989–1995), and whose number of employees is over 100. The number of firms, finally, is 106.

The firms used for our investigation are slightly biased because there are many manufacturing firms that are born and many that die (i.e., new firms and bankrupt ones) in any period. In other words, they are slightly biased towards good firms in performance. Thus, we have to take into consideration the fact that we deal with firms whose business performance is relatively good. We nevertheless investigate firms which include both unionized firms and non-unionized firms, and their rate of proportion between unionized and non-unionized is nearly ideal to examine the effect of unions. Another important feature is that the data include a large number of smaller firms. It is likely that the effect of unions appears more apparent and can be drawn more accurately in smaller firms than in larger firms for various reasons. In other words, it is necessary to distinguish between the effect of unions and that of large enterprise for larger firms, as we emphasized the positive correlation between size of firm and unionization rate in larger firms. In sum, our data source is worthwhile to reveal the effect of unions statistically despite a slightly biased nature.

Tables 8.4 and 8.5 show the general features of observations in the data. Table 8.4 presents the distribution of firm sizes in terms of the number of employees, indicating that the smaller the size of firm, the smaller the rate of union density. This is the common characteristic of the union density in Japan. Incidentally, the share of middle-sized firms (i.e., 300–999 employees) is the largest in the sample.

Table 8.4 Distribution of firm sizes

Employees	*Firms*
10–299	22 (20%)
300–999	77 (73%)
1000–	7 (7%)
Total no. of firms	106

Source: Derived from Japan Economic Journal, *Needs-Company Data File.*

Table 8.5 Summary statistics (106 firms times 7 years)

	Unionized (N=471)	*Non-unionized* (N=271)
Per-employee sales	40.00 (24.89)	40.36 (31.75)
Per-hour sales	17706 (1478)	17094 (1647)
Number of employees	712 (1123)	407 (178)
Regular working hours	170.49 (8.47)	179.14 (8.56)
Overtime hours	17.76 (4.91)	17.78 (4.63)
Capital–labour ratio	10.10 (6.736)	10.68 (9.991)
Male average age	38.58 (3.64)	35.74 (3.42)
Female/male ratio	0.375 (0.689)	0.563 (0.640)
Years since establishment	40.39 (14.71)	32.90 (10.60)

Notes: (1) Sales, capital–labour ratio, etc. are measured by one million yen. Working hours are for one month.
(2) Figures in parentheses are estimated standard errors.

The original data source does not report the value-added figure, and thus we use sales values to represent the measure of production: more concretely, the figure of per-hour sales values which are calculated by the following formula.

Per-hour sales = Total sales/Number of employees times working hours (regular working hours plus overtime hours)

Alternatively, we use also per-capita sales values. Table 8.5 shows that there is no difference between unionized firms and non-unionized firms regarding per-hour or per-capita sales values. At a glance it implies no difference in productivity between them. The number of employees in a firm is larger in unionized firms than in non-unionized firms.

It is appropriate to take into account working hours as labour input since there is significant difference in working hours between unionized firms and non-unionized firms, as found in Chapter 6. Working hours must be taken into account as one of the control variables. We use figures of working hours in *Monthly Labour Statistics* published by the Ministry of Labour because our data source does not report any figures of working hours.

Table 8.5 presents the fact that male average age is older in unionized firms than non-unionized firms. It does not necessarily imply, however, that older ages are equivalent to longer job tenure in a firm, if the rate of labour turnover is common between two categories of firms. Tomita (1993) and Tachibanaki and Noda (1993) showed that the rate of separations in unionized firms was lower than in non-unionized firms, so it is assumed that the retention rate is higher in unionized firms. Therefore, it is possible to conclude that average older age implies longer job tenure in unionized firms. Finally, non-unionized firms show a higher rate of female employees in total employees than unionized firms, implying that it is hard to organize a labour union if a firm has many female employees.

8.4.2 Empirical result

The following fixed effect model is adopted to deal with the endogeneity problem:

$$\ln S/L_{it} = f\,(\alpha_i, Union_{it}, \ln L_{it}, \ln K/L_{it}, Age_{it}, Fem_{it}, Fa_{it}, Boom)$$

where

$\ln S/L$: sales values/(employees times working hours), or sales/employees

ln$L$: labour input, either employees times working hours, or employees
lnK/L: capital–labour ratio
Union: a union dummy, 1; unionized, 0; otherwise
Age: average male employees in a firm
Fem: the proportion of female employees over male employees
Fa: years since a firm was established
α_i signifies the i-th firm's peculiar effect, implying that each firm differs in management capability, employee quality, and others.
The subscript i signifies firm, and t signifies the year specific effect.

A book value of fixed asset is used to represent capital. Labour input uses two definitions. The first is employment times working hours, while the second is employment only. Sales value is deflated by the wholesale price index for the respective industry, and capital is deflated by the wholesale price index for capital goods.

Since the original data source does not include job tenure of employees, both average age of male employees and proportion of female employees over male employees are used to represent some degree of firm-specific human capital. For the former (i.e., age), it indicates both general and firm-specific human capital. If a labour union increased productivity of an employee through firm-specific human capital, a union dummy variable interacted with age would show a positive sign. Incidentally, the simple correlation between age and job tenure for male employees, which was calculated for firms with 100–990 employees in the 1994 *Wage Structure Survey*, is 0.856.

The proportion of female employees is intended to represent the difference between men and women as for their human capital investment. Since the separation rate for female employees is normally higher than for male employees, it is likely that an employer does not invest (i.e., no provision of training) in female employees. Therefore, if the proportion of female employees in the firm was higher, it would imply a negative effect on productivity. Thus, the coefficient of the proportion of female employees would be negative. However, if a union demands more investment in female employees than in male employees because of unions' adherence to identity and principle, a union dummy variable interacted with the proportion of female employees may show a positive value.

Table 8.6 shows the empirical result which took into consideration the effect of working hours. It is found by looking at equation (1) that the union dummy variable interacted with age is positive, while the union dummy variable without any interaction shows a negative effect. The result implies that age affects productivity positively in unionized

Table 8.6 Estimated production functions (Dependent variable: logarithm of per-hour sales, Labour: employees times hours)

	(1)	*(2)*	*(3)*
ln*L*	−0.133**	−0.112**	−0.147**
	(2.335)	(1.965)	(2.558)
lnK/*L*	0.141**	0.141**	0.151**
	(5.669)	(5.692)	(6.109)
Union	−0.620**	−0.750**	−0.832**
	(2.010)	(2.414)	(2.696)
Age	−0.015	−0.011	−0.017
	(0.356)	(0.267)	(0.412)
Fem	−0.076	−0.310**	0.293**
	(1.322)	(2.705)	(2.254)
Fa	0.033**	0.032**	0.034**
	(8.791)	(8.849)	(9.428)
Union × Age	0.017**	0.017**	0.018**
	(2.000)	(2.048)	(2.249)
Union × Fem		0.309**	0.294**
		(2.256)	(2.256)
Union × Boom			0.046**
			(3.619)
Adj R^2	0.957	0.950	0.951
Hausman value	67.98	67.68	77.09
Probability	0.000	0.000	0.000

Notes: (1) Figures in parentheses are estimated *t*-values.
(2) * implies statistical significance at the 0.1 level, and ** at the 0.05 level.

firms, while it has no effect on productivity in non-unionized firms. It is possible to understand that the effect on productivity associated with human capital investment is higher in unionized firms than in non-unionized firms.

The union dummy variable is negative with statistical significance, implying the effect of unions on productivity when the average age of male employees is zero. This estimated value suggests that the effect is 3.6 per cent higher for unionized firms than for non-unionized firms. Basically, it was obtained by the following formulation: $\exp(-0.620+0.017 * 38.58)-1$ where -0.620 is the estimated coefficient of the union dummy, 0.017 is that of the interaction term of union dummy and age, and 38.58 is the estimated average age of male employees in unionized firms. As the retention rate of employees in firms increases, the effect on productivity increases. The result here indicates that the age of 36.47 is the turning point; namely the effect on productivity is positive over that age, and negative under that age. The similar calculation suggests that about 70 per cent of unionized firms have a positive effect on productivity.

Equation (2) includes the interaction term of the proportion of female employees and union dummy in addition to the interaction of age and union dummy. The result on the union dummy and its interaction with age is the same as that in equation (1). Although the proportion of female employees is negative with statistical significance, its interaction with union dummy is positive with statistical significance. By considering the magnitude of the estimated coefficients, it is possible to conclude that an increase in female employees in a firm has a negative effect on productivity in non-unionized firms, while it has no effect in unionized firms because its negative effect is cancelled out. The realistic values of both average age of male employees and proportion of female employees suggest that productivity in unionized firms is 2.9 per cent higher on average than in non-unionized firms.

Equation (3) introduced a boom year dummy for 1988–1990, and its interaction with a union dummy, in order to examine the relationship between business cycles and the effect of unions. The estimated coefficient of the interaction term is positive with statistical significance, implying that the negative effect of unions in boom years is reduced. The calculated result suggests that productivity is 0.1 per cent lower in unionized firms in recession years than in non-unionized firms, while it is 4.5 per cent higher in boom years. We estimated a similar model which added the last year's market share in the industry as an independent variable, as Brunello (1992) adopted. No significantly different implication from this study regarding the effect of unions was obtained, although the empirical result is not provided to save space.

Finally, it is noted that the estimated coefficient on Hausman's statistics supports the validity of the fixed effect model in this panel data analysis. Since all equations in Table 8.6, i.e., equations (1), (2) and (3), satisfy the above, the estimated result regarding the effect of unions is robust.

Table 8.7 shows the estimated result for the model, which does not consider the effect of working hours. Equation (1) suggests that productivity in unionized firms is 2 per cent higher than non-unionized firms. Equation (2) indicates that it is 4.8 per cent lower in recession years, while it is 2.4 per cent higher in boom years. These results are consistent with the result which took into consideration the effect of working hours. It is finally noted that the fixed effect model produced a reliable result in Table 8.7.

Table 8.7 Estimated production functions (Dependent variable: logarithm of per-employee sales, Labour: employees)

	(*1*)	(*2*)
ln*L*	−0.240**	−0.370**
	(3.532)	(5.975)
ln*K*/*L*	0.175**	0.148**
	(6.653)	(6.173)
Union	−0.892**	−0.899**
	(2.742)	(3.016)
Age	−0.012	−0.008
	(0.278)	(0.200)
Fem	−0.251**	−0.193*
	(2.039)	(1.720)
Fa	0.013	0.023**
	(1.610)	(6.651)
Union × Age	0.021**	0.020**
	(2.401)	(2.565)
Union × Fem	0.270**	0.212*
	(1.980)	(1.700)
Union × Boom		0.072**
		(6.006)
Adj R^2	0.942	0.951
Hausman value	49.05	42.45
Probability	0.000	0.000

Notes: (1) Figures in parentheses are estimated *t*-values.
(2) *implies statistical significance at the 0.1 level, and ** at the 0.05 level.

We estimated the other model, which controlled for the contribution of the size of the firm. It is common sense that there is a positive correlation between unionization rate and firm size in Japan. Thus, it is preferable to control for the size of firm in order to distinguish between the pure effect of unions and the effect of firm size. This control also enables us to take into consideration the fact that more firm-specific human capital is invested in larger firms. We eliminated firms whose number of employees is over 1,000. All eliminated firms are unionized, and the average number of employees per unionized firm is 473, the average male age is 38.72, and the average proportion of female employees is 0.347.

Table 8.8 shows that the interaction between union dummy and age is positive, the one between union dummy and the proportion of female employees is positive, and the one between union dummy and boom years' dummy is positive. The effect of the union dummy is

Table 8.8 Estimated production functions for firms with less than 1000 employees (Dependent variable: logarithm of per-hour sales, Labour: employees times hours)

	(1)	(2)	(3)
ln*L*	−0.089	−0.006	−0.104*
	(1.471)	(1.016)	(1.700)
lnK/*L*	0.135**	0.138**	0.148**
	(5.233)	(2.308)	(5.778)
Union	−0.665**	−0.760**	−0.830**
	(2.028)	(2.308)	(2.545)
Age	−0.030	−0.030	−0.038
	(0.654)	(0.662)	(0.831)
Fem	−0.044	−0.344**	−0.314**
	(0.697)	(2.500)	(2.307)
Fa	0.031**	0.029**	0.032**
	(7.788)	(7.770)	(8.422)
Union × Age	0.018**	0.017**	0.018**
	(1.990)	(1.950)	(2.095)
Union × Fem		0.371**	0.352**
		(2.444)	(2.344)
Union × Boom			0.050**
			(3.707)
Adj R^2	0.949	0.949	0.950
Hausman value	59.71	61.13	69.76
Probability	0.000	0.000	0.000

Notes: (1) Figures in parentheses are estimated *t*-values.

(2) * implies statistical significance at the 0.1 level, and ** at the 0.05 level.

negative. All coefficients are statistically significant. The property regarding the signs of these coefficients after controlling for the size of firm is the same as that before the control. Equations (1) and (2) indicate that productivity in unionized firms is higher by 3.1 per cent and by 2.7 per cent, respectively, while equation (3) indicates that it is lower by 1.1 per cent in recession years, and higher by 3.9 per cent in boom years. Again, there is no difference between before-control and after-control for firm size, and the Hausman statistics supports the relevance of the fixed effect model.

8.5 Concluding remarks

This chapter examined the effect of union voices on productivity for listed firms and unlisted firms separately. Different measures to indicate productivity were used between listed firms and unlisted firms; value-added per employee for the former, and sales per employee for the latter. There were also some differences in both the form of production function and the estimation method.

The estimated result suggested that there was a significant difference in productivity between unionized firms and non-unionized firms. Such a difference appeared due largely to the fact that trade unions can encourage better communication opportunities between management and employees through various channels. We presented several channels in Chapters 6 and 7 because unionized firms can have a stronger influence on the voices than non-unionized firms. Then, it was concluded that such voices could guarantee and support a cooperative behaviour of both management and employees. This chapter examined in particular the role of firm-specific human capital, which is able to raise employees' productivity, and proposed that unions were effective in increasing the amount of firm-specific human capital of employees by reducing the number of separations from the firm. Finally, it is noted that we obtained consistent results for both listed firms and non-listed firms.

9
The Effect of Trade Unions on Labour Shares and Industrial Relations

9.1 Introduction

The purpose of this chapter is to estimate the effect of trade unions on the labour share over the value-added by applying panel data of firms by industries. The labour share here implies labour's procurement when the value-added is distributed between labour and capital.

It is possible to conceive of two channels through which trade unions have some effects on the determination of labour share. The first is the effect of trade unions on wages, and the second is the effect of trade unions on productivity. Let us consider the extreme case in which the former is zero, while the latter is positive. It is quite likely that the combined effect of the two effects on the labour share would be negative because employees contributed to a firm but the contribution was not rewarded fully. It was the firm or the capital which gained. The other extreme case would be where the former is positive, while the latter is zero. In this case the combined effect would be positive. The above two examples suggest to us that the power balance between an employer (or more broadly, capital side) and its employees is crucial in determining the effect of trade unions on the labour share. The purpose of this study can be described as the estimation of this power balance.

There are no studies in Japan which have estimated the effect of trade unions on the labour share quantitatively, although there are several studies which have estimated the effect of trade unions on wages, and on productivity. Typical examples are Tachibanaki and Noda (1993), Tsuru and Rebitzer (1995), Noda (1997) and others for the former, and Muramatsu (1984), Noda (1997a) and others for the latter. Needless to say, the content of this book in former chapters examined these issues, and we presented our view. The overall consensus based on these studies is as follows: the effect on wages is negative, while the effect on productivity is positive. Brunello (1992) is the exception for the effect on productivity. Assuming the above consensus, it is possible to guess that the combined effect of trade unions is negative on the labour share. We should like to confirm whether or not this conjecture is correct.

9.2 Theory of collective bargaining and the effect on labour shares

There are several economic theories which examine the effect of trade unions on several economic variables, or depict the behaviour of trade unions. Several examples are (1) a monopsony union model which attempts the maximization of wages of members, (2) a median voter model, or (3) the maximization of the utility function whose arguments are both wages and employees, etc.

The useful theory or idea which can be applied to the issue of the effect of trade unions on the labour share, is the collective bargaining under asymmetry information between an employer and employees. Asymmetry information implies that an employer can know the firm's conditions such as financial conditions, profits, productivity, market condition, etc., while trade unions or employees cannot know them easily. Alternatively speaking, unions' capability of obtaining information on the firm's conditions is quite limited.

Tracy (1987), and Abowd and Tracy (1989) presented the role of asymmetric information in the working of collective bargaining, and concluded that the agreement between an employer and employees at collective bargaining is not determined by the power balance between them but is determined by the degree of information asymmetry. Labour disputes such as strikes and disruptions are used when trade unions want to acquire information on profits and business conditions of the firm because they only have vague information. In other words, if trade unions had accurate and reliable information on the firm's profits and business conditions, both trade unions and employees would avoid strikes and disruptions, and reach an agreement fairly quickly because both sides know that strikes, etc. are costly. This implies that an employer may be willing to release information on the firm's conditions to trade unions and employees, and may encourage employees to accept lower wages when the firm's current condition is not good.

This kind of arrangement supports mutual understanding and trust between an employer and employees, and encourages goal alignment of the firm. Both employer and employees believe that strikes and disruptions damage the firm's competitive power in the industry. At the same time, employees recognize that lowering the wage payment will help the firm's bad performance, and will guarantee the long-term benefits of employees in the final event. A firm which holds a large number of longer-tenured employees is more likely to have the above feature because these employees lose considerably if they leave the firm. In other words, the firm which has a strict internal labour market supports the above feature.

There is a plenty of evidence that information is shared between an employer and employees in Japan. Shirai (1983), for example, proposed that information released by an employer to employees at the collective bargaining session, or more correctly at the work council (or joint consultation) meeting, was as follows: the current business conditions and problems facing the firm, possible desirable policies to solve such problems, management planning, investment planning, transfer of new technology, new factories or offices which are planned by the firm, manpower planning, employment and working conditions, etc.

Shimada (1983) separates the work council meeting from the annual spring offensive (collective bargaining), and presents the fact that the former normally precedes the latter. The collective bargaining session is a formal meeting between an employer and a trade union. In particular, the employer side wants to have the work council meeting when it is anticipated that the usual collective bargaining in spring will not proceed well in view of the firm's unfavourable conditions in sales, profits, financial conditions, etc.

There are several studies which have examined the economic effect of the work council, or information-sharing, on various variables quantitatively. Morishima (1991a,b) estimated the effect of information-sharing on the increase in wages and industrial relations in general under the condition of information asymmetry by applying cross-section data on firms. He obtained the following result: the higher the information-sharing between an employer and employees, the shorter the duration of wage bargaining and the lower the agreed wage payments. He supports the implication of information-sharing. Suruga (1998) shows that employment adjustments, i.e., discharges or layoffs, are less common in the firm where the work council is organized between an employer and employees.

A work council is normally organized in a firm where a trade union is organized, although a trade union is more formal than a work council. We understand, nevertheless, that the role of a work council and that of a trade union are nearly the same in reality. Consequently, information-sharing, which was explained for the role of a work council, can be applied also to the relationship between an employer and a trade union.

Going back to the case of labour shares, we can find several studies of empirical analyses on the effect of trade unions on the labour shares. Kalleberg *et al.* (1984), Henley (1987) and Macpherson (1990) are typical examples.

Kalleberg *et al.* (1984) analyzed the data on American printing industries for 1946–78, and found that the effect of trade unions on the labour shares was positive, although the effect was in a decreasing trend. Henley (1987) proposed the positive effect for the American manufacturing industries in 1972. Macpherson (1990) added several personal characteristics and establishments' size for control purposes and found the positive effect of trade unions on the labour share.

We have already described several studies in Japan regarding the effect of trade unions on both wages and productivity, and presented our conjecture, based on these studies, that the negative effect of trade unions on the labour share would be plausible. Morishima (1991a,b) found, based on his information-sharing and cross-section study, that the effect of trade unions on the firm's profits and productivity was positive, while it was negative on the labour cost (i.e., labour share). The purpose of this chapter is to estimate the effect of trade unions on the labour share, by applying time-series data by industries and employing different explanatory variables. One feature of this study is to use panel data for 19 years and 12 manufacturing firms rather than cross-section data which were commonly applied in the literature.

9.3 Time-series movements in labour disputes and labour shares

It would be useful to recognize what happened to the movement in labour disputes and labour shares in the past. We examine three variables which can represent the condition of labour disputes: (1) the rate of labour disputes, which is measured by the number of labour disputes over total number of employees *Union 2* (per million employees), (2) the participation rate of labour disputes, which is measured by the number of participants in labour disputes over total number of employees *Union 3* (per cent), and (3) the rate of loss by labour inputs, which is measured by the number of days lost over the total number of employees (per one-hundred days) *Union 4*, in addition to the usual

Table 9.1 Time-series changes in various measure of labour disputes and labour share

	Union 1	*Union 2*	*Union 3*	*Union 4*	*Labour share*
1966	37.4	0.95	15.7	15.0	36.8
1967	35.4	1.03	7.3	12.6	35.3
1968	35.5	1.00	9.5	15.6	34.5
1969	36.2	1.33	9.9	20.7	35.0
1970	35.5	1.37	10.3	19.7	36.2
1971	37.3	1.62	10.1	26.6	35.6
1972	37.8	1.55	9.5	20.7	37.3
1973	35.7	1.58	9.0	16.0	37.8
1974	37.0	2.68	17.3	37.1	40.5
1975	38.0	2.18	13.9	33.4	44.9
1976	38.2	1.85	8.2	13.0	43.3
1977	38.2	1.25	3.7	5.7	42.4
1978	38.1	1.09	3.1	3.9	40.1
1979	36.6	0.79	1.7	2.7	39.4
1980	35.9	0.77	2.8	3.9	39.4
1981	35.7	0.63	1.5	2.0	39.2
1982	36.2	0.55	1.5	1.9	39.3
1983	36.1	0.49	1.1	1.3	39.4
1984	35.4	0.37	0.9	1.0	38.1

Source: *Survey on Labour Disputes, fundamental Statistics on Trade Unions,* and *Monthly Labour Statistics,* all by Ministry of Labour.

participation, or density rate of trade unions *Union 1*. The original sources of these statistics are (1) *Survey on Labour Disputes*, (2) *Fundamental Statistics on Trade Unions*, and (3) *Monthly Labour Statistics*. All are published by the Ministry of Labour.

We examine, first, labour disputes. Table 9.1 clearly indicates that the rate of labour disputes had increased until 1974, and started to decline from 1975. Although both the participation rate and the rate of days lost had considerable fluctuations during the entire period, they support the trend indicated by the rate of disputes. The most impressive observation is that the rate of participation and the rate of days lost per one-hundred days are very small in the second half of the 1970s and the first half of the 1980s. It would be possible to conclude that there have been no obvious labour disputes since 1976 which would affect the loss of labour input.

Why had labour disputes disappeared in Japan? It is our understanding that the number of labour disputes would decline, if the degree of information-sharing between an employer and employees were increasing. We can provide two evidences to support our opinion.

The first evidence is that the rate of establishments which have work councils over total establishments had increased from 62.8 per cent in 1972 to 72.0 per cent in 1984 according to *Survey on Communications in Industrial Relations*. This data source shows, moreover, that the increase was from 76.6 per cent to 87.9 per cent for unionized firms, and from 31.3 per cent to 40.7 per cent for non-unionized firms during the same period. We notice a considerable increase in the number of work councils.

The second evidence is given by several case studies. For example, Sato and Umezawa (1983) found that the frequency of meetings between an employer and employees had increased by 65.2 per cent since the first oil-crisis, i.e., 1973–74, and the amount of information shared between them had increased by 66.0 per cent. The information includes management policies and planning, firm's current business conditions on sales, production and profits, etc. It can be concluded that information-sharing among employers and employees has increased since the first oil-crisis and subsequent economic recession.

What happened to the movement in the labour share? It has been in a decreasing trend since 1975 when it showed the highest rate, namely 44.9 per cent. Nishimura and Inoue (1994) presented three empirical results regarding the estimated labour shares which are derived from the following three data sources: *Survey on Corporated Firms, Survey on Industry (Firms), Survey on Individual Firms' Data.*

Their results can be summarized as follows. First, the increase in the labour share in the manufacturing industries during the middle of the rapid economic growth era and afterwards is explained by its increase in larger firms. The labour share in smaller firms has been almost constant. Second, the increase in the labour shares in larger firms is due largely to the increase in the fixed part of wage costs. Third, the fluctuation in the mark-up rate which is defined by the market price over unit cost accounts for the fluctuation in the labour shares.

Incidentally, Nishimura and Inoue found a result similar to our study, namely that 1975 was the peak year of the labour shares in both larger and smaller firms. The labour statistics published by the Ministry of Labour shows that the wage increase in 1974 *Shunto* (spring offensive) was 32.9 per cent, a very high rate, while it was 5.83 per cent in 1979, a fairly low rate. We notice that the determination of wages was considerably flexible in response to a change in the general economic condition. See, for example, Tachibanaki (1987) about flexibility in wage payments.

These results suggest that both the labour share and the labour disputes had increased until the first oil-crisis, when they started to decline.

Also, Yoshikawa (1993) showed that the labour share in the macroeconomy was at a peak in 1975, and has been in a decreasing trend since then. This turning point in 1975 corresponds to the beginning of the declining trend in the union density rate (i.e., participation rate).

It may be concluded based on the above observations that the first oil-crisis is the turning point which distinguished between the increasing rate in both labour disputes and union participation, and the decreasing rate in them. Labour unions, or employees began to accept a decrease in the growth rate in wage payments, and thus a decline in the labour shares. These decreases are caused partly by information-sharing between employers and employees, which was installed and encouraged by a change in macroeconomic conditions. In view of these changes this empirical study distinguishes the sample period between before oil-crisis and after oil-crisis.

It should be useful to refer to a study performed by Oh (1997) who investigated the relationship between labour disputes, and wages and/or prices for the immediate post-war period (1947–1954). He estimated the relationship among the above variables for monthly data. He concluded that the effect of labour disputes was positive on the increase in wage payments, while the effect on the spiral relationship between wages and prices was very marginal. The most important reason for the above finding is that the effect of labour disputes on wages works only for the temporary part of wages, but not for the permanent (or regular) part. Mizuno (1985) also proposed that the effect of labour disputes on wages was positive only for bonus payments, but not for monthly wage payments during the period of rapid economic growth.

9.4 Functional form and data

The adopted functional form for investigating the effect of trade unions on labour shares is as follows:

$$W/Y_{it} = \alpha_i + \alpha_1 K/L_{it} + \alpha_2 K/Y_{it} + \alpha_3 CR_{it} + \alpha_4 SIZE_{it} + \alpha_5 RD_{it} + \alpha_6 UNION_{it}$$

where W/Y, the dependant variable, indicates labour share. This is measured by total wage payments over gross value-added. The explanations of independent variables are as follows. α_i is the industry specific effect. K/L: capital–labour ratio measured by tangible fixed assets over number of employees. K/Y: capital–output ratio measured by tangible fixed assets over value-added. CR: concentration rate in the industry measured by total sales values of firms with employees larger than 1,000 over total sales values in the entire industry. $SIZE$: firm size measured by the number of employees who work in firms with more than 1,000 employees over the number of employees in the industry. The data source of these figures is *Survey of Industry* published by the Ministry of International Trade and Industry. *RD*: R&D expenditure measured by expenditures on research and development over total sales values in the industry. This variable comes from *Survey on Science and Technology* published by the Science and Technology Agency.

Several other variables are added as follows. *AG*: average age of employees in the industry. *FR*: the ratio of female employees over male employees. *SC*: the ratio of male university graduates over male employees. These variables are obtained from *Wage Structure Survey* published by the Ministry of Labour.

The reasons for introducing these variables are fairly straightforward. These variables are expected to affect the determination of labour shares. Since the labour shares are the ratio of the numerator (wage payments) over the denominator (value-added), we consider variables which are assumed to give an influence on either wages or value-added.

The expected sign condition of each variable is as follows. K/L is positive. K/Y is either positive or negative. *CR* is positive. *SIZE* is positive. *RD* is positive. It would not be necessary to explain the reasons why the above sign conditions are expected.

Several labour variables may require some explanations. *AG* is positive because the seniority wage payment system in Japan pays higher wages to older employees than to younger employees. *FR* is negative because a wider wage gap between males and females gives lower total wage payments to females when the female ratio is higher. *SC* is negative because male university graduates normally receive higher wages.

It is important to point out that the purpose of taking into account these variables is not to find out the sign and/or the significance (i.e., the effect) of each variable, but is to control for the influence of these variables in order to reveal the pure effect of trade unions on labour shares. In other words, the variable which was introduced previously is assumed to affect the determination of labour shares. Thus, it is desirable to eliminate the contribution of each variable in order to draw the pure effect.

We now give a few notes about the estimation method. First, we adopt a fixed effect model. Thus, the data are basically a panel basis, implying that the data include both cross-section (i.e., different industries) and time-series nature. Thus, the subscript i signifies industry, while the subcript t signifies time (i.e., year). Second, we apply two methods in representing each variable. The first is an unadjusted variable (i.e., not log-transformed), and the second is log-transformed.

Finally, it is necessary to explain how the effect (or the power) of trade unions is measured. Since this variable is so important in this study, we adopt the following four alternative measures. *Union* 1 is measured by the union participation rate in the industry. It does not necessarily imply the following proposition: 'the higher the participation rate is, the stronger the union power is'. Union 2 is measured by the frequency of labour disputes. This measurement is, in fact, indicated by the ratio of the number of labour disputes in the industry over the total number of employees in the industry. *Union* 3 is measured by the ratio of the number of participants in labour disputes in the industry over the total number of employees. *Union* 4 is measured by the rate of loss in working days by labour disputes in the industry over the total number of employees. The final three measures, which take into consideration the aspect of labour disputes, are expected to indicate the degree of information-sharing, or the extent of cooperativeness between employers and employees.

9.5 Empirical results

Table 9.2 gives the summary statistics of the variables used in this study. We interpret the empirical results mainly based on the estimated equations for the fixed model which used the panel data by industrial level.

Tables 9.3 and 9.4 show the estimated results for the pre-oil-crisis, namely 1966–74. It is found, based on not-log-transformed data, that the union participation rate did not have any effect on the labour shares.

Table 9.2 Summary statistics

	Average	*SD*
Union 1	36.70	1.054
Union 2	1.210	0.600
Union 3	7.210	5.163
Union 4	13.30	11.08
K/L	4.134	3.547
K/Y	0.721	0.307
Concentration	0.496	0.196
Firm size	0.412	0.176
Age	35.23	2.886
Female ratio	0.430	0.488
Male university ratio	0.116	0.050
Labour share	0.385	0.028

Source: *Surveys of Industry*, Ministry of International Trade and Industry. We use also data source in Table 9.1.

Table 9.3 The effect of trade unions on labour shares (1966–74), not log-transformed

	(1)	*(2)*	*(3)*	*(4)*
K/L	−0.052*	−0.079**	−0.059**	−0.053*
	(1.700)	(2.565)	(2.048)	(1.811)
K/Y	0.466**	0.485**	0.456**	0.422**
	(3.291)	(3.492)	(3.390)	(3.285)
CR	−0.070	−0.054	−0.055	−0.060
	(1.011)	(0.796)	(0.819)	(0.902)
RD	0.013	0.013	0.001	0.047
	(0.648)	(0.650)	(0.094)	(0.001)
SIZE	0.024	0.035	0.043	0.049
	(0.188)	(0.650)	(0.338)	(0.385)
UNION 1	−0.137			
	(0.989)			
UNION 2		0.136*		
		(1.772)		
UNION 3			0.141**	
			(2.164)	
UNION 4				0.047*
				(2.058)
AG	−0.027	−0.027	−0.002	0.001
	(0.399)	(0.399)	(0.358)	(0.006)
FR	−0.014	−0.014	−0.015	−0.022
	(0.655)	(0.655)	(0.742)	(1.085)
SC	−0.372	−0.372	−0.378	−0.228
	(0.848)	(0.848)	(0.888)	(0.566)
Adj R^2	0.829	0.834	0.842	0.833
Hausman stat.	0.000	0.000	0.000	0.000

Notes: (1) Figures in parentheses are estimated *t*-values.
(2) * implies statistical significance at the 0.1 level, and ** at the 0.05 level.

It is noted, nevertheless, that all variables associated with labour disputes such as *Union* 2, 3 and 4 are statistically significant and positive.

The results based on log-transformed data show that the union participation rate (i.e., *Union* 1) was not statistically significant, as was true previously. The other three variables, however, such as *Union* 2, 3 and 4 are statistically significant and positive. The estimated coefficients suggest the following numerical effects: the increase in the labour dispute rate by 10 per cent raises the labour share by 0.9 per cent. The increase in the participation rate in labour disputes by 10 per cent raises it by 0.56 per cent, and the increase in the loss rate in working days by 10 per cent raises it by 0.27 per cent.

Table 9.4 The effect of trade unions on labour shares (1966–74), log-transformed

	(1)	(2)	(3)	(4)
ln*K*/*L*	−0.980*	−1.019**	−1.035**	−0.960*
	(9.506)	(10.78)	(11.58)	(10.08)
ln*K*/*Y*	0.930**	0.924**	0.912**	0.891**
	(8.643)	(9.252)	(9.644)	(8.631)
lnCR	0.027	0.028	0.025	0.025
	(0.896)	(0.987)	(0.952)	(0.846)
lnRD	−0.184**	−0.137**	−0.153**	−0.150
	(2.769)	(2.248)	(2.671)	(2.399)
lnSIZE	0.082	0.103*	0.073	0.069
	(1.424)	(1.904)	(1.447)	(1.268)
lnUNION 1	0.097			
	(0.951)			
lnUNION 2		0.092*		
		(3.361)		
lnUNION 3			0.056**	
			(4.530)	
lnUNION 4				0.027*
				(2.640)
AG	0.036**	0.022**	0.014	0.026**
	(3.038)	(2.111)	(1.363)	(2.361)
FR	−0.076*	−0.028	0.012	0.021
	(1.928)	(0.790)	(0.351)	(0.550)
SC	0.519	−0.451	−0.990	−0.323
	(0.741)	(0.660)	(1.467)	(0.457)
Adj R^2	0.943	0.950	0.956	0.948
Hausman stat.	0.000	0.000	0.000	0.000

Notes: (1) Figures in parentheses are estimated *t*-values.
(2) * implies statistical significance at the 0.1 level, and ** at the 0.05 level.

Next, we examine the estimated results for the post-oil-crisis period. They are given in Tables 9.5 and 9.6. The results based on not-log-transformed data indicate that the union participation rate turned out to be statistically significant and positive. This is true for the case of the labour disputes rate. In particular, the two measurements, namely, the participation rate in labour disputes, and the loss rate in working days by labour disputes, are statistically significant and positive.

The estimated results based on log-transformed data suggest the following numerical effects. The increase in the union participation rate by 10 per cent raises the labour share by 2 per cent, the increase in the labour disputes rate raises it by 0.2 per cent, and the increase in the

Table 9.5 The effect of trade unions on labour shares (1975–84), not log-transformed

	(1)	*(2)*	*(3)*	*(4)*
K/L	−0.052**	−0.042**	−0.040**	−0.041*
	(6.331)	(5.218)	(5.343)	(5.508)
K/Y	0.169**	0.201**	0.155*	0.155*
	(2.022)	(2.166)	(1.819)	(1.825)
CR	−0.269**	−0.224**	−0.152	−0.138
	(2.022)	(2.000)	(1.387)	(1.253)
RD	−0.008	−0.009	−0.010	−0.012
	(0.806)	(0.823)	(0.977)	(1.126)
SIZE	0.239**	0.167**	0.130	0.138*
	(3.003)	(2.073)	(1.667)	(1.800)
UNION 1	0.465**			
	(3.212)			
UNION 2		−0.035		
		(0.710)		
UNION 3			0.109**	
			(2.871)	
UNION 4				0.028**
				(2.978)
AG	0.002	0.001	0.007	0.005
	(0.391)	(0.016)	(1.090)	(0.928)
FR	0.027*	0.021	0.030**	0.026*
	(1.868)	(1.414)	(2.048)	(1.787)
SC	−0.356**	−0.370**	−0.389**	−0.359**
	(2.215)	(2.171)	(2.393)	(2.217)
Adj R^2	0.929	0.928	0.935	0.936
Hausman stat.	0.000	0.000	0.000	0.000

Notes: (1) Figures in parentheses are estimated *t*-values.
(2) * implies statistical significance at the 0.1 level, and ** at the 0.05 level.

loss rate by labour disputes raises it by 0.1 per cent. The estimated coefficient, however, for the participation rate in labour disputes is not statistically significant.

The most important finding regarding the difference in sampling periods is considerable decreases in the estimated coefficients for union participations and labour disputes in the post-oil-crisis period. Also, the absolute values in the union participation rate, the labour disputes rate, the participation rate in labour disputes, and the loss rate in working days by labour disputes, decreased considerably from the pre-oil-crisis period to the post-oil-crisis period. All these results imply that the labour shares were influenced negatively, and thus that they decreased considerably.

Table 9.6 The effect of trade unions on labour shares (1975–86), not log-transformed

	(1)	(2)	(3)	(4)
lnK/L	−0.579**	−0.562**	−0.553**	−0.533*
	(9.904)	(11.50)	(10.73)	(10.17)
lnK/Y	0.799**	0.643**	0.629**	0.650**
	(15.27)	(13.35)	(12.45)	(12.97)
lnCR	−0.148**	−0.051	−0.037	−0.049
	(2.237)	(0.817)	(0.591)	(0.766)
lnRD	0.025	−0.049	−0.047	−0.004
	(0.717)	(1.262)	(1.192)	(0.125)
lnSIZE	0.181**	0.158**	0.157**	0.148**
	(4.847)	(4.113)	(4.033)	(3.740)
lnUNION 1	0.220**			
	(2.413)			
lnUNION 2		0.023**		
		(1.990)		
lnUNION 3			0.009	
			(1.412)	
lnUNION 4				0.010**
				(2.068)
AG	0.029**	0.044**	0.042**	0.043**
	(3.005)	(4.420)	(4.243)	(4.288)
FR	0.082**	0.078**	0.082**	0.087**
	(3.634)	(3.229)	(3.333)	(3.457)
SC	−0.814**	−0.768**	−0.754**	−0.800**
	(3.157)	(2.811)	(2.730)	(2.836)
Adj R^2	0.976	0.972	0.972	0.970
Hausman stat.	0.000	0.000	0.000	0.000

Notes: (1) Figures in parentheses are estimated *t*-values.
(2) * implies statistical significance at the 0.1 level, and ** at the 0.05 level.

9.6 Discussions on the empirical results

The overall result of this study suggested that the variables associated with labour disputes were positive on the labour shares. Therefore, it is possible to conclude that the increase in labour disputes which occurred during the pre-oil-crisis period raised the labour shares, while the decrease during the post-oil-crisis lowered them. The most important reason for this distinction arises from the fact that a drastic change in the macroeconomic condition caused by the first oil-crisis altered the industrial relations system. It encouraged both employers and employees to have information-sharing, and thus lowered the number of labour disputes.

It should be helpful to refer to the study by Yoshikawa (1993) who investigated the relationship between trade unions and the macroeconomy. He proposed that several notable changes represented by the drastic increase in price levels, the decrease in the growth rate in both the macroeconomy and firms, the necessity of cost reductions for firms, the increase in service industries, and the decrease in the union participation rate during the post-oil-crisis period brought the following change: the rate of increase in per-capita wage is determined and influenced by various factors such as business performance of firms, general price levels, etc. At the same time, he pointed out that although the higher wage elasticity (i.e., the considerably suppressive wage increase) helped to avoid having a higher inflation rate, the decrease in the labour shares, i.e., lowered labour incomes, decreased the household consumption level significantly. This apparently raises the amount of savings, and thus widens the IS imbalance (i.e., higher savings and lower investments) in Japan. A wider IS imbalance induces an increasing amount of surplus in current accounts in foreign trades. He concludes that the lower labour share caused by many factors, including a decrease in the union participation rate and decreases in labour disputes, is responsible for the international macroeconomic conflict between Japan and abroad, in particular the US.

Besides the effect on the macroeconomy it is important to reconsider the impact of the first oil-crisis on industrial relations. The result obtained in this study is consistent with the interpretation given by Morishima (1991a,b) who emphasized a change in industrial relations caused by the oil-crisis and the subsequent lower growth economy. Firms had to respond seriously to a deteriorated change in the macroeconomy. More importantly, trade unions or employees reacted cooperatively to the behaviour of employers. Basically, they did not demand an increase in wage payments, but tended to accept a small increase. This feeling was enhanced by information-sharing on firms' business conditions and cooperative management strategy between employers and employees. It is striking that employers started to release firms' inside information to their employees during this period.

Information-sharing encouraged employees to be more cooperative with their counterpart, and thus to lower their demands to the firm. One of the important outcomes of this cooperative behaviour is a decrease in labour disputes. Of course, we can point out several other examples of cooperative behaviour, as was proposed elsewhere. This cooperative attitude is likely to have decreased the labour share because the increase in wage payments was smaller than that previously.

It should be interesting to inquire into several other studies in order to examine whether or not our hypothesis was true. Ohtake and Tracy (1994) compared Japan and the US regarding the determination mechanism of strikes and other disputes. Although the two countries showed similarities, in the sense that the possibility of agreement between employers and employees was lower during a period of higher unemployment rates or inflation rates, strike activity in Japan tended to occur when uncertainty associated with the macroeconomy rather than firm-specific uncertainty was high. Ohtake and Tracy attribute this propensity in Japan to information-sharing and cooperative behaviour between employers and employees.

Yoshikawa (1993) estimated the wage function for listed firms' micro data. He found that the most important factor which accounted for a fluctuation in real wage figures was the firm's micro condition (i.e., firm's business performance), and the importance of this factor had increased since the first oil-crisis. As Yoshikawa pointed out, the *Survey on Wage Increases* published by the Ministry of Labour indicates that the micro factor (i.e., firm's business condition) was more important than the macroeconomic condition (i.e., general wage level) in the determination of the firm's wage payments after the oil crisis. The result based on the *Survey* shows that the relative weight between the firm's business condition and the general wage level was almost equal (i.e., 50 per cent versus 50 per cent) in the determination of the firm's wages before 1974, while 60–80 per cent for the former versus 20–40 per cent for the latter after 1975.

Koshiro (1988) estimated the wage function, and found that two variables such as the job vacancy and seeker ratio, and the consumer price index, or three variables such as the above two plus the firm's revenue index, were important to explain the determination of macro wage figures after 1974, although only one variable, namely the job vacancy and seeker ratio, was largely sufficient. His result implies that the wage determination system had changed since the first oil-crisis.

The above results, including this study, all indicate that wages have been determined with more flexibility since the oil crisis. In other words, they are more responsive to a firm's business conditions and general economic condition. One of the causes for this change is the fact that information-sharing about the firm's many conditions between employers and employees, or an informal codetermination system between them, has become common.

By combining with several studies such as Muramatsu (1984), Noda (1997) and others which propose that the effect of trade unions on productivity was positive, it is possible to conclude that the labour shares declined considerably because of the very minor increase in wage payments.

9.7 Concluding remarks

This chapter investigated the effect of trade unions on labour shares by applying cross-industry and time-series data. The overall conclusion suggests that variables associated with labour disputes have a positive effect on labour shares in general. An increase in labour disputes before the first oil-crisis raised the labour shares, while a decrease in labour disputes after it lowered the labour shares. One of the reasons for this change is the fact that information-sharing between employers and employees and informal labour's participation in management lowered the rate of labour disputes after the oil-crisis, and thus encouraged employees to accept a lower increase in wage payments. Needless to say, the most important factor which forced a change in labour's attitude was the general deterioration of economic conditions after the oil-crisis.

This study paid no attention to the difference in firm sizes. It is an important to inquire into the different effect of trade unions by size of firms in view of considerably different degrees of union densities by size of firm. Nishimura and Inoue (1994) found that labour shares differed considerably by size of firm. Thus, it is possible to anticipate that the effect of trade unions on labour shares and income distribution would differ according to size. This is a future work.

10 Concluding Remarks

Various issues on the effect of trade unions in Japan have been examined in this book. The end of each chapter presented a summary of the results obtained in each chapter. Therefore, we avoid repeating the conclusions reached in each chapter. It would nevertheless be useful and helpful to readers if several characteristics and features of this book were described briefly. More specifically, new ideas and methods, and original contributions to the literature, which we hope will be our main message, are presented briefly.

We begin by describing new ideas and methods. First, the Japanese institutional characteristics, in particular enterprise unionism, were taken into account explicitly when the effect of trade unions was assessed. The role of enterprise unionism was evaluated both positively and negatively, and the economic reasons and interpretations were given regarding the positive aspect and the negative aspect.

Second, we constructed a recursive type of model to investigate the effect of trade unions. At the same time, we introduced an intermediary variable called the voice of employees, and quantified it to be used in the econometric approach. The causation proceeds in the following way by combining a recursive type of model and an intermediary variable, namely the voice of employees; trade unions → employee voices → various economic effects.

Third, we paid attention to the preference of non-union members as well as union members We are inclined to be concerned only with the attitude of union members when we examine the movement in union participation rates. The attitude of employees in non-unionized firms is equally crucial because they may organize a new union in future. It is of interest to know whether or not they are inclined towards union activity and organizing a new union.

Fourth, we were concerned with the expectation of both union members and non-union members. What kind of goals do employees expect among a large number of working conditions such as wages, working hours, etc., through union activities? What are the important working conditions among many? Do they find that trade unions are effective in achieving such goals? If yes, why are unions successful in achieving them? If not, do they want to leave trade unions? We examined these issues.

Fifth, we paid particular and careful attention to the effect of trade unions on wages in view of the fact that it is the most popular subject in the world. Nearly equal attention was paid to various variables regarding working conditions, including unions' egalitarianism among members and the relationship between management and employees. The latter aspect could provide us with a new interpretation of the firm's performance.

Sixth, we were concerned with the effect of trade unions on both the productivity of a firm and the determination of labour shares. These two subjects are particularly important because they can partly explain the performance not only in each firm but also in the macroeconomy in general. If the effect were positive, it would imply that both employers and employees (i.e., trade unions) behaved cooperatively. If it were negative, they were likely to be opposed each other.

We would like to point out several new observations made in this book which we hope will contribute to the economic analysis of trade unions. First, one of the important reasons why the rate of union participations in Japan has declined constantly is the attitude and preference of employees, in particular non-union members. Suppose that employees want to raise their wage payments. There are two policy alternatives. The first is to exert strong union power which demands higher wages from their employer. The second is to work hard and thus to attempt to be promoted to a higher position in the firm where a higher wage is paid. This does not rely, of course, on union power. Most employees in Japan, including non-union members, prefer the second to the first. Therefore, they are not interested in union activity in general. This feature obviously does not encourage an increase in the number of unionized firms and thus the rate of union participations.

Second, it is very important to recognize the fact that there is a high correlation between the size of firm and the rate of unionized firms in Japan. The larger the firm, the more likely it is to have a union. Also, nearly all employees, except for those in managerial positions and those who are not regular employees, belong to only one union in the firm. All kinds of workers regardless of their profession belong to that union. This feature is called enterprise unionism.

These two facts, namely (i) the high correlation between firm size and unionization, and (ii) enterprise unionism, are crucial in evaluating the role of trade unions in industrial relations in Japan and the economic interpretations. First of all, we have to separate the effect of being a large firm which gives a comparative advantage in its production and sales activity in the industry, and the effect of trade unions, in order to derive a pure effect of trade unions. At the same time, we can understand that it is necessary and sufficient to compare unionized firms and non-unionized firms in order to derive a pure effect of trade unions on various economic variables. Second, enterprise unionism provided not only employees but also employers with a unique incentive which leads the employees' working attitudes, and thus the firm's performance, to a favourable position. We will describe the second matter below again.

Third, it is important to evaluate the role of satisfaction when we investigate employees' attitudes to their working activity. Satisfaction here signifies whether employees are satisfied with several working conditions, but unsatisfied with other conditions. Employees determine their working behaviour often based on their psychological judgments on employers' treatment of employees. In particular, we found that the propensity to stay in the firm was influenced by this satisfaction variable. The propensity to stay here implies only employee's preference, and does not describe any actual separation.

Fourth, it was found that female wage payments were marginally higher in unionized firms than in non-unionized firms, while male wage payments showed the inverse relationship. It would be preferable, however, to conclude that there is no difference in wage payments for both males and females judging from the fact that no statistically significant coefficients of the union dummy variable in the wage function were found. This is confirmed even in the case in which a simultaneity (i.e., endogeneity of union status) problem and/or a sample selection problem were taken into account. The fact that there is no significant union effect on wages in Japan is consistent with the common understanding that the positive effect is observed only in the UK and the US, and thus that in many countries there is no significant union effect on wages. Careful economic studies in Japan supported the above opinion.

Fifth, we found that the problem of simultaneity (i.e., endogeneity of trade union status) and/or the problem of sample selection bias were not serious at least in Japan, when we were concerned with the effect of trade unions on various working conditions including wages. This was confirmed by various statistical testing. Therefore, it is feasible to rely on a single equation where a union dummy variable is included as an independent variable without taking into consideration a simultaneous equation model and/or a correction of a sample selection bias for the investigation of the effect of unions at least in Japan.

Sixth, our new variable, namely the voice of employees, was successful in investigating the role of unions on various economic conditions in the framework of an econometric approach. This variable was introduced as an intermediary variable which transmits employees' preferences to various economic variables. Incidentally, the econometric approach adopted here is a recursive one. The voice of employees was the dependent variable in the first equation, and it was used as the independent variable in the second equation. In sum, the joint consideration of a recursive model and the voice of employees was a useful method in the investigation of the effect of trade unions.

Seventh, when we are concerned with non-wage working conditions such as severance payments, paid holidays, overtime working hours, etc., or with management matters such as training, firm's welfare system such as housing and medical insurance, daily management conditions, transfer of employees within the firm and outsourcing, promotion policy of employees, top-level management policies and planning, etc., a different story from the effect of trade unions on wages was obtained. In other words, some of the above non-wage working conditions and management matters were found to be influenced by the voice of employees, and eventually, favourably by trade unions. 'Favourably' here implies the positive contribution of trade unions to the performance of the firm such as, for example, productivity. Consequently, it was possible to conclude that trade unions served as institutions which contributed to the better working of industrial relations in Japan and thus the better performance of the firm. A lower rate of separation from the firm in unionized firms through the voice of employees was also additional evidence to support the merit of enterprise unionism.

Eighth, we proposed that the principal reason for the above favourable effect of trade unions was caused by the feature of enterprise unionism in Japan. We offered three alternative judgments which could support the above proposition. First, enterprise unionism is able to provide both employers and unions (employees) with cooperative behaviour. Second, Japanese management is excellent, and Japanese unions (employees) are too weak. This may be the result of enterprise unionism. Third, both management and unions (employees) are excellent because of enterprise unionism. We felt that the first judgment was the most plausible interpretation in the sense that both employers and unions (employees) were cooperative because of enterprise unionism in order to increase the firm's performance and thus the competitive power of the firm.

Ninth, we presented empirical evidence by estimating production functions such as that trade unions raised firms' productivity. At the same time, we also estimated the determination of labour shares, and found that unions behaved quite cooperatively in dealing with labour shares. We offered again the importance of enterprise unionism to explain the above. At the same time, we emphasized the usefulness of better communication between employers and employees, information-sharing between them on the firm's economic conditions, and the contribution of specific human capital to account for the above findings.

Bibliography

Abowd, J. and J. Tracy (1989), 'Market Structure, Strike Activity, and Union Wage Settlements', *Industrial Relations*, vol. 28, no. 2, Spring, pp. 227–50.

Addison, J. T. and B. T. Hirsch (1989), 'Union Effects on Productivity, Profits, and Growth: Has the Long Run Arrived?', *Journal of Labor Economics*, vol. 7, January, pp. 72–105.

Benson, J. (1994), 'The Economic Effects of Unionism on Japanese Manufacturing Enterprises', *British Journal of Industrial Relations*, vol. 32, pp. 1–21.

Blanchflower, D. G. and R. B. Freeman (1992), 'Unionism in the United States and Other Advanced OECD Countries', *Industrial Relations*, vol. 31, Winter, pp. 56–79.

Booth, A. (1995), *The Economics of the Trade Union*, Cambridge: Cambridge University Press.

Brown, C. and J. L. Medoff (1978), 'Trade Unions in the Production Process', *Journal of Political Economy*, vol. 86, June, pp. 355–78.

Brunello, G. (1992), 'The Effect of Unions on Firm Performance in Japanese Manufacturing', *Industrial and Labor Relations Review*, vol. 45, April, pp. 471–87.

Calmfors, L. (1993), 'Centralization of Wage Bargaining and Macroeconomic Performance: A Survey', *OECD Economic Studies*, vol. 21, pp. 161–91.

Calmfors, L. and J. Driffil (1988), 'Bargaining Structure, Corporatism and Macroeconomic Performance', *Economic Policy*, vol. 6, pp. 13–62.

Dickens, W. and J. S. Leonard (1985), 'Accounting for the Decline in Union Membership, 1950–80', *Industrial and Labor Relations Review*, vol. 38. pp. 323–34.

Duncan, M. and D. E. Leigh (1985), 'The Endogeneity of Union Status: An Empirical Test', *Journal of Labor Economics*, vol. 3, July, pp. 385–402.

Farber, H. S. (1986), 'The Analysis of Union Behavior', in O. Ashenfelter and R. Layard (eds), *Handbook of Labor Economics*, vol. II, Amsterdam: North-Holland.

Farber, H. S. (1990), 'The Decline of Unionization in the United States', *Journal of Labor Economics*, vol. 8, no. 1, part 2, pp. S75–S105.

Freeman, R. B. (1980a), 'The Exit–Voice Tradeoff in the Labor Market: Unionism, Job Tenure, Quits, and Separations', *Quarterly Journal of Economics*, vol. 94, June, pp. 643–74.

Freeman, R. B. (1980b), 'Unionism and the Dispersion of Wages', *Industrial and Labor Relations Review*, vol. 34, no. 1, October, pp. 3–23.

Freeman, R. B. (1982), 'Union Wage Practices and Wage Dispersion within Establishment', *Industrial and Labour Relations Review*, vol. 36, pp. 3–21.

Freeman, R. B. (1984), 'Longitudinal Analyses of the Effects of Trade Unions', *Journal of Labor Economics*, vol. 2, January, pp. 1–26.

Freeman, R. B. (1986), 'The Effect of the Union Wage Differential on Management Opposition and Organising Success', *American Economic Review*, vol. 76, pp. 92–6.

Freeman, R. B. (1990), 'Employer Behavior in the Face of Union Organizing Drives', *Industrial and Labor Relations Review*, vol. 43, pp. 351–65.

Freeman, R.B. and R. S. Gibbons (1995), 'The Decline of Centralized Collective Bargaining', in R.B. Freeman and L.F. Katz (eds), *Differences and Changes in Wage Structures*, Chicago: University of Chicago Press, pp. 345–71.

Freeman, R. B. and M. E. Kleiner (1990), 'The Impact of New Unionization on Wages and Working Conditions', *Journal of Labor Economics*, vol. 8, no. 1, part 2, pp. S8–S25.

Freeman, R. B. and J. L. Medoff (1984), *What Do Unions Do?*, New York: Basic Books.

Freeman, R. B. and M. Rebick (1989), 'Crumbling Pillar? Declining Union Density in Japan', *Journal of the Japanese and International Economies*, vol. 3, pp. 578–605.

Goldfeld, M. (1987), *The Decline of Organized Labor*, University of Chicago Press.

Gordon, R. J. (1982), 'Why U.S. Wage and Employment Behaviour Differs from That in Britain and Japan', *Economic Journal*, vol. 92, pp. 13–44.

Hashimoto, M. (1990), *The Japanese Labor Market in a Comparative Perspective with the United States*, Kalamazoo: Upojohn Institute.

Henley, A. (1987), 'Trade Unions, Market Concentration and Income Distribution in United States Manufacturing Industry', *International Journal of Industrial Organization*, vol. 5, no. 2, pp. 193–210.

Hirsch, B. T. (1982), 'The Interindustry Structure of Unionism, Earnings, and Earnings Dispersion', *Industrial and Labor Relations Review*, vol. 36, no. 1, October, pp. 22–39.

Ishida, M. (1990), *Social Sciences of Wages: Japan versus the U.K.*, Chuo Keizai-sha (in Japanese).

Ishida, M. (1992), 'An Analysis of Wage Determination, Merit System and Industrial Relations', in T. Tachibanaki (ed.), *Assessment, Promotion, and Wages*, Tokyo: Yuhikaku (in Japanese).

Ishikawa, T. (1982), 'Dual Labor Market Hypothesis and Long-Run Income Distribution', *Journal of Economic Development*, vol. 9, no. 1, August, pp. 1–30.

Ishikawa, T. (1996), 'Interindustry and Firm Size Differences in Job Satisfaction among Japanese Workers', in T. Tachibanaki (ed.), *Labour Market and Economic Performance: Europe, Japan and the USA*, London: Macmillan Press, chapter 7, pp. 183–215.

Kalleberg, A. L., M. Wallace and L. E. Raffalovich (1984), 'Accounting for Labor's Share: Class and Income Distribution in the Printing Industry', *Industrial and Labor Relations Review*, vol. 37, no. 3, pp. 386–402.

Kochan, T. A., H. C. Katz and R. B. McKersie (1986), *The Transformation of American Industrial Relations*, New York: Basic Books.

Koike, K. (1962), *Wage Negotiations in Japan*, Tokyo: University of Tokyo Press (in Japanese).

Koike, K. (1977), *Trade Unions at Shop Floors and Participation : A Comparison of Industrial Relations between Japan and the U.S.*, Tokyo: Toyokeizai-shimposha (in Japanese).

Koike, K. (1983), 'Trade Unions and White-collar Employees', in Japan Institute of Labour (ed.), *Industrial Relations in the 1980s* (in Japanese).

Koshiro, K. (1983), *Japan's Industrial Relations*, Tokyo: Yuhikaku (in Japanese).

Koshiro, K. (1988), 'Changes in Industrial Structure and Industrial Relations', *Monthly Journal of the Japan Institute of Labour*, no. 346,pp. 29–39 (in Japanese).
Kumazawa, M. (1982), 'Post-war History of Work-Places: Human Management in the Iron and Steel Industry and Trade Unions', in S. Shimizu (ed.), *Post-War History of Trade Unionism*, Tokyo: Nihonhyoronsha (in Japanese).
Lewin, D. (1984), *Opening the Books: Corporate Information Sharing with Employees*, New York: The Conference Board.
Lewis, H. G. (1986), 'Union Relative Wage Effects', in O. Ashenfelter and R. Layard (eds), *Handbook of Labor Economics*, vol. II, Elsevier Science Publishers, pp. 1139–81.
Lincoln, J. R. and A. L. Kalleberg (1990), *Culture, Control and Commitment: A Study of Work Organization and Work Attitudes in the United States and Japan*, Cambridge: Cambridge University Press.
Macpherson, D. A. (1990), 'Trade Unions and Labor's Share in U.S. Manufacturing Industries', *International Journal of Industrial Organization*, vol. 8, no. 1, pp. 143–51.
Metcalf, D. (1989) 'Water Notes Dry Up: The Impact of the Donovan Reform Proposals and Thatcherism at Work on Labour Productivity in British Manufacturing Industry', *British Journal of Industrial Relations*, vol. 27, pp. 1–31.
Metcalf, D. (1993), 'Industrial Relations and Economic Performance', *British Journal of Industrial Relations*, vol. 31, pp. 255–83.
Mizuno, A. (1985), 'Wage Flexibility and Employment Fluctuation', in R. Nakamura, S. Nishikawa and Y. Kosai (eds), *Economic Systems in Modern Japan*, Tokyo: University of Tokyo Press, pp. 50–73 (in Japanese).
Moene, K. O., M. Wallerstein and M. Hoel (1993), 'Bargaining Structure and Economic Performance', in R. Flanagan *et al.* (eds), *Trade Union Behaviour, Pay Bargaining and Economic Performance*, Oxford: Clarendon Press.
Morishima, M. (1991a), 'Information Sharing and Collective Bargaining in Japan: Effects on Wage Negotiation', *Industrial and Labor Relations Review*, vol. 44, no. 3, April, pp. 469–85.
Morishima, M. (1991b), 'Information Sharing and Firm Performance in Japan', *Industrial Relations*, vol. 30, pp. 37–61.
Morishima, M. (1992), 'Use of Joint Consultation Committees by Large Japanese Firms', *British Journal of Industrial Relations*, vol. 30, pp. 405–24.
Muramatsu, K. (1984), 'The Effect of Trade Unions on Productivity in Japanese Manufacturing Firms', in M. Aoki (ed.), *The Economic Analysis of the Japanese Firms*, Amsterdam: North-Holland Publishing Company, pp. 103–23.
Muramatsu, K. (1993), 'Job Satisfaction and Trade Unions', in T. Tachibanaki (ed.), *Economics of Trade Unions: Expectation and Reality*, Toyokeizai-shimposha, chapter 5, pp. 89–106 (in Japanese).
Nakamura, K., H. Sato and T. Kamiya (1988), *Are Unions Really Beneficial?*, Sogo Rodo Kenkyusho (in Japanese).
Nakata, Y. (1995), 'Wage Determination in the Auto-industry: Wage Differentials Across Firms', in Ministry of Labour (ed.), *A Change in Employment System and Labour Market*, Osaka: Kansai Economic Research Center (in Japanese).
Nishimura, K. and A. Inoue (1994), 'Labour Shares in Japanese Manufacturing Industries since the Period of Rapid Economic Growth: Dual Structure and

Imperfect Competition', in T. Ishikawa (ed.), *Japan's Income and Wealth Distribution*, Tokyo: University of Tokyo Press, pp. 79–106 (in Japanese).
Noda, T. (1997a), 'The Effect of Unions on Firm Productivity for Unlisted Firms', *The Monthly Journal of the Japan Institute of Labour*, no. 430, pp. 36–47 (in Japanese).
Noda, T. (1997b), 'Wage Structure and Enterprise Union', *JCER Economic Journal*, no. 35, December, pp. 26–44 (in Japanese).
Noda, T. and T. Tachibanaki (1998), 'Unions, Strikes and Labour Shares,' mimeo (in Japanese).
Odaka, K. (1984), *Analysis on Labour Market*, Tokyo: Iwanami-shoten (in Japanese).
OECD (1994), *Employment Outlook*, Paris: OECD.
Oh, S. (1997), 'Labour Disputes, and Wage-Price Spiral in Japan', *Keizai Kenkyu*, vol. 48, no. 3, pp. 252–61
Ohashi, I. (1993), 'Trade Unions as Public Goods', in T. Tachibanaki (ed.), *Economics of Trade Unions: Expectation and Reality*, Toyokeizai-Shimposha, chapter 8, pp. 151–72 (in Japanese).
Ohashi, I. and T. Tachibanaki (eds) (1998), *Internal Labour Markets, Incentives and Employment*, London: Macmillan Press.
Ohta, S. and T. Tachibanaki (1998), 'Job Tenure versus Age: Effect on Wages and the Implication of Consumption for Wages', in I. Ohashi and T. Tachibanaki (eds), *Internal Labour Markets, Incentives and Employment*, London: Macmillan Press, chapter 3, pp. 49–77.
Ohtake, F. and J. S. Tracy (1994), 'The Determinants of Labour Disputes in Japan: A Comparison with the U.S., in T. Tachibanaki (ed.), *Labour Market and Economic Performance : Europe, Japan and the USA*, London: Macmillan Press.
Oswald, A J. (1985), 'The Economic Theory of Trade Unions: An Introductory Survey', *Scandinavian Journal of Economics*, vol. 87, no. 2, pp. 160–93.
Rengo (1989), *Report on Trade Union Policy* (in Japanese).
Robinson, C. (1989), 'The Joint Determination of Union Status and Union Wage Effects: Some Tests of Alternative Models', *Journal of Political Economy*, vol. 97, June, pp. 639–67.
Robinson, C. and N. Tomes (1984), 'Union Wage Differentials in the Public and Private Sectors: A Simultaneous Equations Specification', *Journal of Labor Economics*, vol. 2, January, pp. 106–27.
Sakamoto, M. (1993), 'Trade Union Activity in Future', in T. Tachibanaki (ed.), *Economics of Trade Unions: Expectation and Reality*, Toyokeizai-Shimposha, chapter 7, pp. 131–49 (in Japanese).
Sano, Y. (1969), *An Econometric Analysis of Wage Determination*, Toyokeizai-shinposha (in Japanese).
Sato, H. and H. Umezawa (1983), '*Voices of Unions and type of Unions*', in Japan Institute of Labour (ed.), *Industrial Relations in the 1980s*, pp. 34–49 (in Japanese).
Shimada, H. (1983), 'Wage Determination and Information Sharing: An Alternative Approach to Income Policy?', *Journal of Industrial Relations*, vol. 25, no. 2, pp. 177–200.
Shirai, T. (1983), 'A Theory of Enterprise Unionism', in T. Shirai (ed.), *Contemporary Industrial Relations in Japan*, Madison, Wis.: University of Wisconsin Press.

Suruga, T. (1998), 'Employment Adjustment in Japanese Firms: Negative Profits and Dismissals', in I. Ohashi and T. Tachibanaki (eds), *Internal Labour Markets, Incentives and Employment*, London: Macmillan Press, chapter 9, pp. 196–224.

Tabata, H. (1991), 'Japanese Society and Industrial Relations', in Institute of Social Science at University of Tokyo (ed.), *Modern Japanese Society, vol. 5*, Tokyo: University of Tokyo Press (in Japanese).

Tachibanaki, T. (1982), 'Further Results on Japanese Wage Differentials: Nenko Wages, Hierarchical Positions, Bonuses, and Working Hours', *International Economic Review*, vol. 23, no. 2, pp. 447–61.

Tachibanaki, T. (1986), 'On Economics of Trade Unions', Research Project on the Quality of Unemployment and Employment, Kansai Economic Research Center, mimeo (in Japanese).

Tachibanaki, T. (1987a), 'Labour Market Flexibility in Japan in Comparison with Europe and the U.S.', *European Economic Review*, vol. 31, pp. 647–84.

Tachibanaki, T. (1987b), 'The Determination of the Promotion Process in Organizations and of Earnings Differentials', *Journal of Economic Behaviour and Organization*, vol. 8, pp. 603–16.

Tachibanaki, T. (1988), 'Education, Occupation, Hierarchy, and Earnings', *Economics of Education Review*, vol. 7, pp. 221–9.

Tachibanaki, T. (1992a), 'Why Are Wages in Finance and Insurance Industry in Japan So High?', in A. Horiuchi and N. Yoshino (eds), *Financial Analysis for Modern Japan*, Tokyo: University of Tokyo Press (in Japanese).

Tachibanaki, T. (1992b), 'Higher Land Price as a Cause of Increasing Inequality: Changes in Wealth Distribution and Socio-economic Effects', in J. O. Haley and K. Yamamura (eds), *Land Issues in Japan: A Policy Failure*, Seattle: Society for Japanese Studies.

Tachibanaki, T. (ed.) (1993), *Economics of Trade Unions: Expectation and Reality*, Toyokeizai-Shimposha (in Japanese).

Tachibanaki, T. (1996a), *Wage Determination and Distribution in Japan*, Oxford: Clarendon Press.

Tachibanaki, T. (1996b), *Public Policies and the Japanese Economy: Savings, Investments, Unemployment, Inequality*, London: Macmillan Press.

Tachibanaki, T. (ed.) (1998), *Who Runs Japanese Business?: Management and Motivation in the Firm*, London: Edward Elgar.

Tachibanaki, T. and T. Noda (1993), 'The Economic Effect of Trade Unions', in T. Tachibanaki (ed.), *Economics of Trade Unions: Expectation and Reality*, Tokyo: Toyokeizai-shimposha, chapter 10, pp. 195–216 (in Japanese).

Tachibanaki, T. and T. Noda (1996), 'Enterprise Unionism: The Japanese System at Work', *Economic Policy*, no. 23, October, pp. 469–85.

Tachibanaki, T. and S. Ohta (1994), 'Wage Differentials by Industry and the Size of Firm, and Labour Market in Japan', in T. Tachibanaki (ed.), *Labour Market and Economic Performance: Europe, Japan and the USA*, London: Macmillan Press, chapter 3, pp. 56–92.

Tachibanaki, T. and A. Taki (2000), *Capital and Labour in Japan: The Functions of Two Factor Markets*, London: Routledge.

Takagi, I. (1982), 'Right-Wing in Enterprise Unionism in Japan and Labour Policy', in S. Simizu (ed.), *Post-War History of Trade Unionism*, Tokyo: Nihonhyoronsha (in Japanese).

Tomita, Y. (1993), 'The Rate of Separation and Voices of Trade Unions', in T. Tachibanaki (ed.), *Economics of Trade Unions: Expectation and Reality*, Toyokeizai-shimposha, chapter 9, pp. 173–93 (in Japanese).

Tracy, J. S. (1987), 'An Empirical Test of an Asymmetric Information Model of Strikes', *Journal of Labor Economics*, vol. 5, no. 2, pp. 149–73.

Tsuru, T., D. Hayashi and J. B. Rebitzer (1993), 'The Determinants of the Declining Union Participation Rates', *Japan Institute of Labour Report*, no. 43 (in Japanese).

Tsuru, T. and J. B. Rebitzer (1995), 'The Limits of Enterprise Unionism: Prospects for Continuing Union Decline in Japan', *British Journal of Industrial Relations*, vol. 33, no. 3, September, pp. 459–92.

Wang, Xinmei (1997), 'Labor Disputes and the Wage–Price Spiral in Japan: 1945-1954', *Economic Review*, vol. 48, no. 3, pp. 252–61 (in Japanese).

Yoshikawa, K. (1993), 'Trade Unions and Macroeconomy', in T. Tachibanaki (ed.), *Economics of Trade Unions: Expectation and Reality*, Toyokeizai-shimposha, chapter 11, pp. 217–36 (in Japanese).

Index